The King's Cup
Rugby's First 'World Cup'

Howard Evans and
Phil Atkinson

St David's Press
Cardiff

Published in Wales by St. David's Press, an imprint of

Ashley Drake Publishing Ltd
PO Box 733
Cardiff
CF14 7ZY

www.st-davids-press.com

First Impression – 2015

ISBN 978-1-902719-44-3

British Library Cataloguing-in-Publication Data.
A CIP catalogue for this book is available from the British Library.

Typeset by Replika Press Pvt Ltd, India
Printed by Akcent Media, Czech Republic

Contents

Preface

'Rugby and Society in 1919: a look back...and forward'

The guns had fallen silent in Europe in November 1918. However, the long Versailles discussions which would apportion blame and damages and map the borders – and, fatefully, the future conflicts – of Europe and beyond, were not concluded until the summer of 1919. In the interim, many of the Allied armed forces remained in uniform. Those who were shipped to Britain, awaiting release and in many cases a return 'Down Under', were able, in the case of talented rugby men, to enthusiastically participate in the King's Cup.

So it was that before Lloyd George and Co. put pen to paper in the Hall of Mirrors, what has been described as the nearest thing to a first rugby World Cup had taken place in Britain, with a quickly devised and arranged competition ending with what was to prove so regular a feature of the subsequent century: New Zealand at the top of the rugby pile.

Rejoicing at the end of the Great War, with its dreadful cost in all senses, was to be tempered not only by the pain experienced by so many left behind, but also by the effects of the influenza pandemic (which was responsible for more deaths than the war), and by the growing realisation that Britain's land and homes were not, after all, going to prove 'fit for the heroes' who had welcomed the PM's promise.

Nothing was going to be the same again, historians were to later agree, but the military's sporting organisers were certainly going to try to keep the flag flying in the immediate post-Armistice months. The Cup to which George V was asked to give his name (and clearly-genuine support) was in effect a topped-up, higher-powered version of the games played during the previous four years by a small host of military sectional, divisional, 'trench' and other teams, often from the colonials' ranks, against club, regional or even national teams.

Raising (in order) recruits, morale (the teams' and the people's), crowds and charitable funds, these had effectively served their purpose, and while the standard may have been well below that of the official 'Original' All Blacks, Wallabies and Springbok tourists of 1905, 1908 and 1906/1912, the promoters and propagandists of these wartime clashes were quick to bill the visitors as 'New Zealand' etc, even when few former caps were taking the field.

Often, though, stars of rugby league as well as union in the forces from home and abroad did feature, interest was clearly genuine, and the Army Service Corps 'side of all the talents' gathered at Grove Park in London by Major R V Stanley (of Oxford University's 'Stanley's XV fame) was unbeatable for a time. The ASC team included some of the cream of rugby league: Huddersfield's Harold Wagstaff, Douglas Clark, Ben Gronow and Albert Rosenfeld, Rochdale's Joe Corsi and league cap Ernest Jones, together with Oldham's Frank Holbrooke.

Army Service Corps XV, Grove Park, London: 'All the talents, Union and League'

They hammered almost every other team in the south of England, including Australian and NZ services sides, winning 25 out of 26 games with tallies of 1,110 points to 41. Their only defeat was a 6-3 loss to a United Services side which included eight rugby union internationals and a young Wavell Wakefield, plus Wigan's Billy Seddon and Leeds' Willie Davies. A similar and longer-lasting side was assembled at the Devonport Royal Navy depot, again with over half the team being drawn from the 'Northern Union'.

When 'Wales' took on the Barbarians in Cardiff's 1915 fundraiser, the programme billed the visitors as 'England' (who won the game) and real care must be exercised in researching the validity of the titles claimed in many of the lesser clashes. An October 1918 'Barbarians v New Zealand' programme listed in the National Museum of NZ archives aroused disconcerted interest and surprise: until the accompanying image proved it to have been the Torquay Barbarians, raised from a selection of local sides!

The King's Cup, though, was to be far nearer to the real thing, with a wider choice of available personnel from the armed forces of most of the world's leading rugby playing nations, plus Canada, and crowds to match. The details of the tournament, with its 'Mother Country' name for the British side seeming most appropriate in light of the loyal response of so many from the corners of Empire, are fully laid out elsewhere in these pages.

However, the competition clearly hoped to restore a degree of sporting excitement and excellence, as well as providing welcome distraction for the participants awaiting repatriation – *'so many soldiers, so few ships!'* – and the action was shared around the country. In a year when League soccer would not restart until August, when there was no Open Golf Championship and no Varsity Boat Race, many will have welcomed the experience of quality sport and some confirmation that things might get back to normal.

Normality, though, was hardly the order of the day in 1919. In transport, for instance, Bentley Motors were incorporated, Alcock and Brown made the first non-stop transatlantic flight, east from Newfoundland to Ireland, while the British airship R34 made the first transatlantic flight by a dirigible, west from Scotland to New York. Oh, and the German fleet was scuttled at Scapa Flow.

Frustration was not the sole preserve of the German admiral who took that decision: some British troops refused to sail back to France or be sent to oppose the Soviet revolution, police went on strike, Canadian troops at Kinmel Park Camp in North Wales and at Epsom mutinied and rioted, with deaths at both, and as Irish Home Rule arguments raged Éamon de Valera, the leader of Sinn Féin, and two other prisoners escaped from Lincoln Prison helped by Michael Collins.

On 'Peace Day', July 19, victory parades had been held across Britain but disgruntled rioters including ex-servicemen burnt down Luton Town Hall. Edwin Lutyens' London Cenotaph was unveiled and later the first Remembrance Day was observed with two minutes silence at 11:00 am on November 11. The Third Anglo-Afghan War ended with Afghanistan gaining more control of their foreign affairs, Viscountess Nancy Astor became the first woman to take her seat in the House of Commons and meat rationing ended in time for Christmas.

Amongst the year's books were those by a trio who would be firmly remembered a century on: John Maynard Keynes' with his *Economic*

Consequences of the Peace; Siegfried Sassoon: *War Poems* and P. G. Wodehouse's early collection – *My Man Jeeves*.

It was the last named who wrote of rugby: *"I know that the main scheme is to work the ball down the field somehow and deposit it over the line at the other end, and that, in order to squelch this programme, each side is allowed to put in a certain amount of assault and battery and do things to its fellow-man which, if done elsewhere, would result in fourteen days without the option, coupled with some strong remarks from the Bench."*

Births included several who were to loom large in the fields of arts, literature and sport, including Margot Fonteyn, Beryl Reid, Donald Pleasence, Jon Pertwee, Doris Lessing, Iris Murdoch, Bob Paisley and, in New Zealand,

'Ranji' Wilson, of West Indian heritage: barred from touring S Africa

Parekura Tureia, a Maori: also unwelcome in South Africa

Edmund Hillary. There was an unclimbable Everest, though, for those who looked for change at the RFU. They and other unions quickly restored the status quo regarding rugby league (Northern Union) players, who *'could play rugby union in the services only if they did not play or sign for NU'* while in the forces, and clubs could not meet Service teams containing NU players. The WRU, while awarding caps, were apparently wary of playing against any New Zealand former professionals before their 3-6 defeat at Swansea in April 1919. Such fears received short shrift from some observers, who underlined the sacrifices made for the 'Mother Country' by amateur and professional alike. In fact, behind the scenes Horace Lyne of the WRU had tried to persuade the International Board to agree to the reinstatement of league men to the union game after hostilities, but got no support.

Hopes of a more 'level playing field' having been produced by the war were not justified, it seems. The NU supporter (quoted by Tony Collins) who asked: *"As the war in this country is being fought on democratic lines, so will the future government of this land be on more democratic lines. There will be far less class distinction than we have been accustomed to. Merit will be recognized. Is it not possible that this may obtain in our sports?"* was to be disappointed. The RFU was to be no advocate of social change, but the very opposite.

Meanwhile, the King's Cup winners, New Zealand, were invited to tour South Africa, who asked that no 'coloured' players be included, so Parekura Tureia and 'Ranji' Wilson, the brilliant NZ flanker with West Indian heritage, were removed from the team with no demurral from New Zealand. No change there, either, then, for a very long time: as Chapter 7 will detail.

Even 'Votes for Women', hard-earned by the war's end, were for the next decade granted only to women over 30, and indeed 1919 saw some soldiers striking to demand speedier demobilisation and industrial unrest and strikes in rail, coal and cotton workers, expecting their 'hero's reward' (or even less perhaps) became disillusioned. Collins concludes: *"Rugby's example shows that while patriotic war fervor may have suppressed some class antagonisms, basic conflicts remained and rapidly re-emerged post-1918. For English rugby union and its supporters, the Great War did not mark the passing of the old world."*

It was to the Northern Union that all too many of Wales' most promising players were once again to pass over the coming years. From the Welsh game, 'both democratic and amateur', the working rugby man – who was indeed more a part of the union game there than in any other area of these islands – was tempted away from the declining economy of South Wales to the relative riches of rugby league. Scores of Welsh caps, and many more without one, 'Went North' between the wars.

The Scottish Union, dyed in the wool amateurs who refused even to number their jerseys, believed with some cause that Welsh clubs were themselves going down the payments route in an effort to stem the flow. The SRU always seemed to find 'a Welsh problem' (or a NZ one) and it was only the arrival of graduates and professional men amongst the Welsh backs of the 1930s that eased the tartan tension.

It was that social class which had always dominated the game in Scotland, Ireland and much of England. Whereas the Northern Union, with its often working class players and middle class owners had 25 years earlier broken away from the RFU, Wales was able to maintain its allegiance to the 15-man code with a mixture of independence and shamateurism.

Ironically, it was the Welsh-born fly half and captain of England, W.J.A.Davies, the 'Pembrokeshire Petal' in England's rose, who wrote of the RFU in his 1923 book: *"It has been my privilege to meet those in command of Rugby football in this country and nothing has impressed me more than the natural abhorrence of all members to the slightest sign of professionalism or vestige of unfairness. Rugby football is sport, a sport vital for the good of our country, and it is as a sport, and not a business, that it must remain."*

Rugby might have flourished elsewhere, but in the Welsh valleys the industrial decline of the '20s and '30s, the growth of soccer's appeal and the league's siren song found many clubs on their knees – or flat out. Jobs went, gates fell, debts rose, clubs disappeared: for instance, at Rhymney *'a full 1923-24 fixture list was printed, but Brynmawr didn't turn up, 'Billy Abergwili' went north, and the Club went west! Rhymney's season seems to have quite suddenly fallen through the floor'*. So did Wales' efforts against the 1924 All Black 'Invincibles', as they slumped 19-0 at Swansea.

Smith and Williams in their WRU history 'Fields of Praise' found light at the tunnel's end in the contemporaneous growth of schoolboy rugby. It thrilled the old cap Rowe Harding, and that switch from soccer had been a major feature of many English public and grammar schools since 1919, as the middle classes sought the comfort and security of what were seen as rugby's conservative, nostalgic and 'well-mannered' virtues compared with rugby league, soccer and Bolshevism.

A headteacher wrote to The Times: *"Now that all the world is devoting itself to reconstruction, and all institutions are making a new start, is it too much to hope that all schools will consider seriously the adoption of Rugby football as the winter game for all the youth of the nation?"*

Indeed, to a degree this proved a feature in the Rhymney club's own revival by 1933. *'The famous Lewis School Pengam, down valley, and then the local Rhymney Secondary School, 'adopted the oval', and as talented players emerged two local shop owners paid off the £16 debt which had apparently caused the club's demise and supplied them with new kit…'* In the same year Wales were to gain their first win at Twickenham and, two years on, beat the 1935 All Blacks 13-12 at Cardiff.

A year after that, following his 'something must be done' tour, King Edward VIII's departure point from the Valleys (and soon after, the country) was Rhymney Station. Three years later and three miles away, Merthyr Tydfil found a Government Enquiry recommending that the once Iron Capital of the World be closed down and moved to the coast. It wasn't: World War Two arrived instead.

Phil Atkinson
Editor of *'Touchlines'*,
the magazine of the Rugby Memorabilia Society

Acknowledgements

I have always loved watching New Zealand rugby, and thanks in particular to three New Zealanders – Henry Magnussen, John Blackwell and his wife Janet – that interest and urge to research came to include the period before and just after World War One.

The King's Cup of 1919 came into my mind as I have never seen a book written specifically on that competition, and three Welshmen also now stand out for their contributions to it.

They are my former boss, Rob Cole, who thankfully also loves rugby history; John Griffiths, with his unbelievable memory for details and Phil Atkinson of the Rugby Memorabilia Society, Rhymney RFC and formerly of Jesus College, Oxford. Without these three there would be no book.

Phil Atkinson not only contributed the chapter on post-war Britain, but by amazing good fortune turned out to be a former history teacher. He agreed to edit the book, adding many photographs and has generally been a massive driving force, so much so that he became joint-author.

Timothy Auty's contribution was also huge and Dave Fox, Les Williams, Mike Dams, Ray Ruddick and many others were superb.

The competition was played by the men who survived the worst of all wars, but they, like me, would have dedicated it to the many rugger players and officials who died serving their countries.

Sadly, I can find little reference anywhere to many of the Canadian players, other than names and ranks, but I suspect that very few of them ever played the sport again.

I would finally like to gratefully acknowledge the assistance received from Diana McRae and Kirsty Willis of the Alexander Turnbull Library, Wellington, New Zealand, in identifying and securing the necessary copyright clearance for the usage in this book, of the 12 images from the 'Royal New Zealand Returned and Services' Association Collection'.

Howard Evans
Cardiff, October 2015

This book is dedicated to all those who never made it back to play for, watch or learn of the King's Cup, but gave their lives for their countries; and to the huge numbers so badly injured that though they lived, it was with lasting wounds and ongoing nightmares of the terrible conflict in which they had taken part.

Introduction

The Great War had ended. Those rugby players who had survived intact – and indeed, some who had been wounded – returned to Britain to play once again the sport they loved. Britain had not been bombed by German planes in the way that would happen in World War Two, and many had not, for some time fully understood the full extent of the losses and horror on all sides: news was more easily suppressed in days long before television, computers and social media.

Now, though, the country was to see the reality of so many brave young men having died or been so severely maimed as to never be able to carry on their life in the way they had prior to 1914. Nevertheless, some sort of more normal life and sport resumed and taking part in or watching events, such as a rugby match, allowed many to forget for an hour or two the carnage that had gone on.

Many of those who took part in the war had come from the Empire – as was to happen again 20 years later – and those who played rugby from New Zealand, Australia and South Africa, in particular, played in trials, both inside and outside Britain, to represent their country for several months after the armistice prior to returning to their own countries.

I met many of the Kiwis (the NZ Expeditionary Force side) of 1945-46 when they returned for a mid-1990s reunion trip. Among them were great players, capped pre and post War, including Cyril Saxton, Fred Allen, Bob Scott and Jim Sherratt. As they gathered around with Welsh players such as Les Manfield, Maldwyn James, Jack Matthews, Bleddyn Williams and Billy Cleaver, I asked Fred Allen why those New Zealand Army players had not opted to go straight home after years of fighting.

The later Sir Frederick Allen, a NZ captain and coach-to-be, looked at me incredulously and answered for all those standing close by, who nodded as he replied: "Why go home? This was a rugby tour. It was much more important!!" (And he meant it). Yes, at the end of both wars, New Zealanders played in trials in Germany, Austria, France etc. and 'fought' to play in their Services sides: and in both 1919 and 1945, even ex-prisoners of war joined in.

The British public had for the most part been able to watch only Services rugby from 1914 to 1918 (and it was to prove likewise from 1939 to 1945).

Welsh, English, Irish, Scottish, Australian, Canadian, South African and New Zealand players took part, and they, and the watchers, loved it. Rugby league players were allowed in, as long as they were Services personnel, and the rugby was often a joy to behold. Many who played, though, were very shortly to die. At the front, some played their last game just hours before going into battle.

So it was that in March and April 1919, just months after hostilities ended, the competition eventually called the Kings Cup was held, with games in Wales, Scotland and England before a play-off at Twickenham: with the winners to be then challenged by France, also at 'HQ', just three days later.

First, though, we have to return to 1914 and 'the World that Was.....'

Explanatory Notes

Team Listings and Player Positions

The listing of players for each game usually follows the convention of –

Full Back; Right Wing, Outside Centre, Inside Centre, Left Wing; Fly Half, Scrum Half; then the forward pack, generally listed Front Row, Second Row then Back Row: but bearing in mind that specialism was only then developing, and 'Forward' was the usual position listed.

However, due to the use of an alternative system in New Zealand, their teams are listed as follows –

Full Back; Right Wing, Centre, Left Wing; Second Five-Eighth, First Five Eighth, Scrum Half; then the forward pack, with the same qualification as mentioned above.

International Caps and Rugby League Status

Each player is also denoted as to their status concerning international caps or whether they were rugby league players, as follows –

*   capped before World War One
+   capped after World War One
RL   rugby league player

New Zealand Team Names

Prior to the start of the King's Cup, there were a plethora of New Zealand teams that took the name 'NZ Services', but once the team for the King's Cup had been selected in March 1919, it took the name 'NZ Army'. The term New Zealand Army was then retained for the post-King's Cup game against Wales and for the tour of South Africa.

1

Rugby in Wartime

'Our boys will have their game of football under all sorts of conditions'

At 11.00pm on Tuesday, August 4, 1914 came the announcement that "a state of War exists between Britain and Germany." Millions of soldiers, sailors, airmen and civilians were to die in the 52 months of what became known as the Great War, the War to end all Wars and eventually – sadly disproving that hope – World War One.

The long-simmering European tensions and power-struggles found an unwitting trigger in the assassination of Archduke Franz Ferdinand of Austria on June 28, 1914. Within four weeks Austria-Hungary declared war on Serbia, setting off a diplomatic domino effect amongst the major powers.

Germany's entry into Belgium and Luxembourg on their move towards France had brought in Britain, who had already made promises

Rugby Union plays the patriotic card - or poster

WELSH FOOTBALL UNION.

PATRONS:

HIS MAJESTY THE KING.

SIR J. T. D. LLEWELYN, Bart.

NORWOOD,

NEATH, Sept. 4th, 1914.

DEAR SIR,

AT a Meeting of my Committee held at the "QUEEN's" Hotel, CARDIFF, last evening, the following Resolutions were unanimously passed:—

1.—"That this Committee, being of opinion that the interests of our "Country will best be served by discontinuing the Playing "of Football, calls upon all affiliated Clubs to suspend "Fixtures until further advised."

2.—"That we again urge upon all men eligible for service, and "particularly Footballers, the very great importance of at "once placing their services at the disposal of the Military "Authorities, and also desire to point out to others, who "by reason of age or other circumstances are precluded from "enlisting, that great and valuable services may be rendered "by them in volunteering their services to the Authorities "for home duties."

3.—"That we strongly recommend our Clubs to place their Grounds "at the disposal of the Authorities."

Yours faithfully,

Walter E. Rees

SECRETARY.

The Welsh Rugby Union nails its colours to the mast in 1914 (Newport RFC)

to France and Russia. The British Expeditionary Force were decimated as Lord Kitchener's Army volunteered and trained, and the stalemate of trench warfare set in, with the bloodied battlegrounds resembling something many times worse than the Cardiff Arms Park pitch and its renowned mud.

Rugby union was, at the time and since, quick to trumpet its contribution amongst sportsmen voluntarily signing up as recruits for His Majesty's Forces. Indeed, from the young university officer class, so likely to be rugby players, through to the miners and other manual workers of Wales and the North of England for instance, it provided both numbers and poster-propaganda; sometimes in an unseemly contrast to the professionals of soccer and rugby league, to whom sport was their livelihood, rather than a pastime.

Rugby in Britain had halted almost as soon as war was declared and only Army, schools and fund-raising matches for war funds were held, though soccer carried on in a limited fashion. The season that had been due to start in September 1914 had been cancelled but on October 31, 1914 there was a match played at Hove between English and Welsh troops based in Shoreham and Seaford. The English troops won 24-0 (six tries and three conversions) with proceeds being shared between the Funds of the Prince of Wales and the Belgian Refugees.

Rugby men had sometimes signed up for their country after 80 minutes hard sport, and as Neath's fine secretary and historian, Mike Price, said: *"In the immediate mood of euphoria which swept the country, many were motivated to*

The 'Welsh' team at Hove, Oct 14th 1914

The Hove crowd, including recruits. It was 24-0 to England, though, not 54-0!

join up. Perhaps the words of the hardened Neath forward Tim Jenkins summed up their feelings when he wrote from his training camp at Draycott – 'The Germans broke poor Belgium's ground record, but we are going to smash them'. However, things took a turn for the worse as the Western Front settled into attritional trench warfare and the grim reality of industrial war set in."

Indeed, those, capped or obscure, who signed up thinking that they would have a quick foreign adventure and defeat the enemy within months before returning to continue their sporting activities were to be proved tragically wrong. There were many days in France and Belgium where the Allies or the Germans gained only the length of a couple of rugby pitches as each side attacked and counter-attacked in the most dreadful of conditions of mud and machine guns, shells and stench, trench fear and fever, rats and gas.

As Christmas after Christmas – and optimism – passed, from 1915 to 1917 Britain and France suffered more casualties than did Germany. The Battle of the Somme began on July 1, 1916 and that day alone saw the British Army suffer 57,000 casualties, including over 19,000 dead. The full Somme offensive cost Britain 420,000 casualties, with France suffering some 200,000 and Germany about 500,000.

The Allies, and in particular Australia and New Zealand, gained huge pride against the Turks at Gallipoli in 1915, but lost great numbers. Romania joined the Allies in 1916, but it is barely possible to calculate the gigantic

1912: Pym, Pillman & Poulton etc already playing for England, Lewis, Stephens, Coldrick and Co, for Wales

Russian losses before they withdrew late in 1917, and small Serbia lost around 850,000 people. The USA entered the War in 1917 and reinforced the Allies with some 2.8 million troops but Germany came within 75 miles of Paris before being driven back and seeking terms.

Dave Gallaher, All Black captain 1905 ....

Sergeant, World War One, 1916.....

Some six million British men had been in uniform of whom 750,000 were killed, 170,000 were made PoWs and 1,700,000 wounded. Britain and the Dominions had up to 889,000 killed while the German losses were over two million dead. More than 1.4 million French soldiers died while Australia had lost 60,000, Canada 61,000, NZ 16,500, SA 18,500 and the USA over 116,000.

Amongst the dead were many rugby men, including some of the cream of capped players – more than 130 international rugby union players died. Of the 30 who played in the Calcutta Cup match of 1914, seven Scotland and five England players fell, while the 1912 match between Scotland and South Africa also saw 12 lost – nine from Scotland and three from South Africa, for there were also deaths amongst famous caps from far-flung parts of the Empire who voluntarily came to fight. Dave Gallaher, 1905 All Black captain killed at Passchendaele, was the most renowned of those.

By the latest trawl in Nigel McCrery's *'Into Touch'* (he includes a few outside the dateline accepted by others), the tallies saw Scotland having lost the most capped players, 31, England 28, France 21 and Wales 14. (Gwyn Prescott's fine *'Call Them to Remembrance'* does not include Hop Maddock, whose death fell outside the 'deadline' officially imposed). Ireland and New Zealand lost perhaps 13 each, Australia 9, South Africa 5, the British Lions two Englishmen uncapped by their country but having played Test rugby, and the USA one.

Killed on the Western Front, 1917

In Wales, as elsewhere, many miners, policemen and others in 'protected' occupations, who did not have to go to war after conscription replaced voluntary

OGDEN'S CIGARETTES.

H. T. MADDOCKS.

Hopkin Maddock: a cigarette card hero (NB: card is incorrect)

enlistment in 1916, quit their jobs to do so – and many never returned. Of all the lost, the RFU president Arthur Hartley was to say: *"Their supreme sacrifice will not have been in vain if we live nobly and carry into the game this spirit."*

From the Varsities, 55 Rugby Blues (27 Oxford, 28 Cambridge) were killed, plus many more sporting students who had not quite made the first teams. It was estimated that 115 New South Wales players died at Gallipoli, while by 1918 that Union alone had lost 388 players and officials. The impact of WWI on the NSWRU was crippling, and on Queensland, worse. However, a very special consequence of so many NSWRU players going to war was the talent and spirit that was born in the 1st Australian Imperial Force (AIF) Rugby Team that formed in Egypt prior to leaving for the assault on Gallipoli.

'Hop' the war hero: died of wounds 1921

Irish RFU Volunteer Corps Badge

Wallaby and Olympic Gold Medallist Thomas James 'Rusty' Richards wrote in his diary: *'Most of these matches before our soldiers travelled to Gallipoli were played under the shadows of the Great Pyramids, games that meant as much to the players and their keen followers as ever did an international at the Sydney Cricket Ground.'* Rusty went on to write about rugby between the batallions in France: *'Rugby Football matches have now become common amongst the Australian troops whilst resting after a spell in the trenches...for tomorrow they will be en route to the Somme again and the greatest hell ever thought of. But what care they for the morrow, let's find out who are*

la Vie Aérienne

A LA
MÉMOIRE
DE
**MAURICE
BOYAU**

AS
DE L'
AVIATION
DE
GUERRE
∎
**RUGBYMAN
PRESTIGIEUX**
∎
PARRAIN
DE LA
**COUPE
BASTOUL·
SECRESTAT**
CRÉÉE POUR
DÉVELOPPER
L'AVIATION DE
TOURISME, MISE
EN COMPÉTITION
POUR LA PREMIÈRE
FOIS À BORDEAUX

Maurice Boyau, French rugbyman and flying ace: another who fell

the best footballers while there is still time in hand.'

Clubs, meanwhile, suffered hugely, Bristol losing 300 members, while the Old Merchant Taylors' side of 1914 had 13 killed and two permanently disabled. Rosslyn Park's 72 mourned in 1919 have swollen through Stephen Cooper's impressive researches to over 85. London Scottish turned out 60 players for four sides in the spring of 1914, of whom 45 were killed and only one (a prop) was able to play again after hostilities had ended. In all, that club reckoned 103 of their players died, including 17 internationals. Only 29 pre-war players returned to action on the field. The Twickenham field, in the interim, had grazed horses.

They had, though, in some cases seen sporting as well as military action at the front. Games did occur during breaks in the fighting and often sides played without referees. It all helped raise morale and great men who died, such as the hugely-admired England internationals Ronnie Poulton-Palmer and Edgar Mobbs, actually played their final matches in France or Belgium.

Rochdale and England rugby league wing Jack Robinson had commented: *"Our boys will have their game of football under all sorts of conditions"*. Rugby, and more commonly, soccer – as in the famous 'Christmas truce' games – was certainly a welcome and frequent distraction. Jack was badly wounded in 1915, but his words were truly spoken, as rugby balls were shipped out to the front-lines and occasionally kicked high ahead as men went 'over the top': many (balls and men) literally never to be seen again.

As the war dragged on, some senior rugby was played at home, but largely for morale, recruiting and fundraising purposes, with substantial crowds drawn. Rugby league players joined in and were eventually given dispensation to play the union game for the time they were in the Forces.

Aussies behind the lines

Twickenham: fit for grazing, 1915

Twickenham: fit for a King's Cup

Edgar Mobbs, Northampton, England and lasting fame: captain of the Barbarians v Wales 1915

(This was repeated in World War Two and, later, National Service).

On April 17, 1915, for instance, a Wales XV lost 10-26 to the Barbarians' 'Services Team' (although the programme said 'England') at Cardiff Arms Park, *'with receipts claimed at £200 for local military charities, while after the final whistle, 177 were recruited for the Welsh Guards.'*

Wales, led by fiery forward, the Rev Alban Davies, who was already an Army chaplain, did not award caps, and played in white. The Baabaas were in their usual famous black and white hoops in this, one of their six special fundraising and recruiting games that season.

In the team photograph, Tommy Vile, seated alongside his skipper, appears to have a black cat on his lap. If so, it brought little luck, this experienced Wales XV being outplayed despite Davies leading a side made up of 13 capped players and another, Tom Parker of Swansea, who went on to gain 14 caps.

NZ troops train for war - and rugby

The Welch Regiment do the same

And the Scots!

It was really the Barbarians, not England, but that didn't stop the programme producers

Wales v 'England', 1915: the teams

The Barbarians, Cardiff, 1915

The lone player never to win a cap was a Cardiff forward Dan Callan (a Munster Fusilier), who played when Tom Williams of Swansea withdrew. Joseph Quinn, the visitors' Blackrock wing, who had won 15 caps for

Wales, Cardiff, 1915

Ireland, scored two tries and soon afterwards earned a Military Cross. He had scored seven tries in his last five international appearances.

April 17, 1915 – Wales XV 10 Barbarians 26
Arms Park, Cardiff

Wales XV: R Williams; I T Davies, W H Evans, J Wetter, B Lewis; Clem Lewis, T Vile; T Lloyd, Rev A Davies (capt), D Callan, W Jenkins, Percy Jones, D Watts, Edgar Morgan, T Parker.

Tries – B Lewis, I T Davies. **Drop Goal –** Clem Lewis.

Barbarians: G Wood; E Butcher, J Birkett, E Mobbs (capt), J Minch, J Quinn; A Horan, H Higgins; G Roberts, J Partridge, A Bull, A Osbourn, G Kidman, M Atkinson, L Davies.

Tries – J Quinn 2, A Bull, J Minch, A Horan, J Birkett. **Cons –** E Butcher 2, G Roberts 2.

Referee – Mr Bill Douglas of Cardiff, a Barry man who won four caps for Wales in 1886 and 1887. He had refereed four international matches from 1891-1903.

The Welshman who played in the Barbarians side (the 18th of his 19 appearances for them) was actually a South African international! It was Joseph Edward Crawshay Partridge, known as 'The Bird', born in 1879 at Llanthewy Court, Monmouthshire. He went to Dulwich College, and made 188 appearances for Newport in two spells between 1898-1901 and 1904-11. He also played for London Welsh, Blackheath (skipper 1907-8) and Kent, and got an England trial in 1906. He was also to be the referee for the challenge match between the King's Cup winners and France.

Partridge was a lieutenant in the 2nd Batallion, Welch Regiment in the Boer War, and whilst serving played for the Civil Service Rugby Club in Pretoria. In 18 days he played against the 1903 GB side four times, with two wins and a draw: a debut victory in Transvaal's 12-3 win on August 8, another triumph two weeks later by 14-5, a Springbok cap in a 10-10 draw in the First Test and a 15-3 defeat for Pretoria.

Stationed back in London and on a train heading to Scotland with Blackheath in 1906 he apparently had the idea of forming an Army rugby team. He

'Bird' Partridge, born in Wales, trial for England, capped for S Africa

discussed it with his travelling companions and teammates, Lieutenant W S D Craven (Royal Field Artillery) and Lieutenant (later General Sir Clive) C G Liddell (Leicestershire Regiment) and a meeting was held on November 12, 1906 to form the ARU.

'Bird' won Army caps in 1907, '08, '09 (captain) and '10, and won the Army Cup with the Welch Regiment in 1912 and 1913, when they also took the Aldershot Command Cup. Later a lieutenant-colonel, he died in Abergavenny in 1965 at the age of 86 and his cap was presented to the Regimental Museum.

Three of the players that day – Brinley Lewis and Dai Watts of the Wales XV and Edgar Mobbs, the English skipper of the Baabaas – were later to die on the Western Front, while John Minch, the visitors' Irish centre, died as a prisoner of war in World War Two. The Barbarians had just over 200 members on active service, of whom the shocking figure of 63 – over 30% – were killed.

Of the few games played in 1916, usually involving Services teams, there was a 9-7 win for a New Zealand outfit against South Wales at Swansea in November, then at the same venue on Boxing Day a Wales XV drew 6-6 against the New Zealand Services. A return match on February 3, 1917 was cancelled due to bad weather. Australian and NZ troops in training or convalescing also formed teams, some of which, like that from the NZ Codford

Aussies from France 1916

LES AUSTRALIENS GUERRIERS ET SPORTIFS

...and in London. Aussie Rules action, reported in France as rugby.

Camp in Wiltshire, had considerable success: as did Floss, their performing dog!

Floss was a bitch fox terrier from Sir Walter Long's kennels, Towbridge. She was given to Driver Percy E (Ike) Lowndes, who taught her many tricks, and took her round hospitals, camps and even the stage of the London Empire Theatre.

Floss could skip up to 40 jumps on her hind legs over a turning skipping-rope, leap a specially-made hurdle 14 inches high and land on her hind legs. She could pray, go to bed, play a piano, count to five, sit at a table and give orders to the waiter, and take cover in an air raid.

Floss became the mascot of this NZ Army football team. It is the 'Z' of NZ that is visible on her jersey in photographs. She toured in her jersey for the Diggers, and raised hundreds of pounds for disabled servicefolk.

Despite all her good deeds, the quarantine authorities would not let Floss into New Zealand, even though they received a petition signed by 1,000 New Zealand Expeditionary Force men. However, Ike Lowndes smuggled her back to Wellington, where after nine months' quarantine on Somes Island, she was released.

Floss performed for many charities around the North Island. She was a good ratcatcher, too, and is thought to have descendants around Gisborne, where Ike had a soldier's farm for a while.

NZ team from Codford Camp with Floss, their performing dog.

Floss died at the age of 17 about 1935. She was stuffed and kept in a glass case by Mr Lowndes at Eastbourne, then given to the Wellington Returned Servicemen's Association, and later the Auckland R.S.A. Sadly, neither Auckland R.S.A. nor Auckland Museum know where Floss is today.

The fragment of ticket which has survived from the 'Rugby International Match' at Cardiff Arms Park on 24th February 1917 did rather better than the match. Neither it, nor the tour of which it was to be part, took place.

In early February 1917, it had been announced that a team of New Zealand soldiers (the "NZ Trench Team") had been given permission to leave the Western Front to undertake a short tour in Britain. Four fixtures were arranged: the Army Service Corps; New Zealanders in training in

Ticket fragment from an unplayed 1917 clash

THE BATTLE IN THE FOOTBALL FIELD

The war has proved the value of games generally, and of football in particular, as a training for the grim business of the battlefield, and to mark their appreciation of this fact the authorities have permitted a number of New Zealanders to leave the front and play a brief series of games in this country for the benefit of the Red Cross. The tour, which concludes to-morrow (Saturday), began last Saturday with a match at the Athletic Grounds, Richmond, between the New Zealand Trench Team and the Army Service Corps, when the All Blacks were beaten by 21 points to 3.

The Army Service Corps v a New Zealand team, Richmond, February 1917

the UK; Public Schools and Hospitals; and (on 24th February) Wales. The proceeds were to be donated to the British Red Cross and other charities.

However, shortly after, it was announced that due to "unforeseen circumstances" – possibly 'professional' fears after the guarantees demanded, or just reluctance to spare men from the front – the tour had been curtailed, so that Wales game at Cardiff never took place. New Zealanders in training in Britain, of course, continued to play fixtures, and many 'smaller' Services-based games took place around the country in the war's later years.

Competition – between Cardiff and Swansea over hosting such matches, and between soccer and rugby – was never far away, it seems. Recently, the soccer men of Swansea's History Project website, seeking details of a Swans' Easter Monday game in 1918 for which they, coincidentally, had found a ticket, reported as follows: *'....the local paper, the South Wales Daily Post (ancestor of today's Evening Post) failed completely to preview the Swansea Town v the Royal Flying Corps football match. (This was the last game they played as the RFC: on the very day of the match (1ˢᵗ April) the Royal Air Force was created from the R.F.C. and the Royal Naval Air Service).*

At the same time the paper was giving a lot of space to advertising an international rugby game at St. Helen's. This game, between South Wales and New Zealand, was billed as "Easter Monday's Great Game", and the Daily Post laid it on with a trowel about how 'Every penny taken at St. Helen's Football Ground on Easter Monday will help to provide food for starving Welsh prisoners of war in Germany'. The fact that the particular fund to benefit was the Daily Post War Prisoners' Fund may have had something to do with this bias of promotion in favour of the rugby. The rugby and football games had the same kick-off time at 3.30, but it cost 3d more to go into the ground than at the Vetch, with much higher rates for stand seats.

On the following day (2ⁿᵈ April), a column was devoted to reporting on the marvellous game at St. Helen's, how the plucky Welsh players were behind at the end of the first half, but came storming back in the second period to win 13-6. The fact that the New Zealanders had played on the Saturday in Cardiff may have had something to do with this....'

The same sharp source underlines our earlier point on the attraction of sport at the time, that entertainment of any sort was clearly welcome at that stage of the war, as rationing loomed and there were basic shortages across the country – *'potatoes were being delivered to local bakeries as a bread additive to try and improve the quality of loaf produced from home-grown wheat.'*

Thankfully, some of rugby's pre-war stars, along with a host of fine overseas players, who were shortly to permanently return from the trenches proved just the additive to add quality to the sporting fare on offer on Britain's rugby pitches by the end of the year.

2

The Armistice: Rugby Resumes, 1918-19

'They had come to fight and die for us'

On Monday, November 11, 1918 at 5.00 am, the Armistice was finally agreed in a railway carriage at Compiegne, north-east of Paris. The ceasefire came into force six hours later: 11.00 am on the 11th day of the 11th month. Effectively, the war was over.

Some six million British men had been in uniform of whom about 750,000 were killed, 170,000 were made PoWs and 1,700,000 wounded. Britain and the Dominions had up to 889,000 killed while the German losses included over two million dead. More than 1.4 million French soldiers died, while Australia had lost 60,000, Canada 61,000, NZ 16,500, SA 18,500 and the USA over 116,000.

The rest would return, yes: but sadly, as well as those killed, many former players at all levels were so badly disabled or disorientated that they could never play again. Some suffered depression, in a number of cases leading to suicide, and few who experienced those unspeakably bad days and the very worst of conditions could avoid reliving them. Many saw months and years of rehabilitation, successful or otherwise, with the tallies of players fallen in the war never taking into consideration those who suffered years of living hell before an all-too-early grave.

However, rugby was back – albeit not fully at club level until September 1919 – and schools, meanwhile, were in many cases beginning to turn from soccer to rugby. The sporting public in Britain, France and the Empire had been starved of top quality action, and after the Armistice both players and spectators were keen to play and watch some old and many new faces and talents.

As Rhymney RFC's 'History' comments: *"Our skipper, pictured in 1919, was Jack Gardner, who looked hard and lean and doubtless hungry for the five years of rugby 'stolen' by the War. He was to tack them on to the other end of his career by way of recompense!"*

At least he could: there was the stark reminder on numerous war memorials that many players, officials and supporters would never come back, while some who did return were without limbs, or with their minds seriously affected. On Rhymney's memorial alone were 120 names, including 'a very promising young wing' named Billy Parry. A great rugby future had been predicted for him, but it was not to be: *"He laid down his life with a great many of his football friends, as 1914 closed a long chapter of football in the town, but it was to come back into existence after the War ended."*

A smooth resumption of local club rugby was not necessarily an easy task, though, with those losses – human, spiritual and financial – of the war all too real and problematic in many cases, while the years ahead were to be difficult in many areas.

As previously mentioned, in the Welsh valleys and beyond, unemployment, frustration, strikes, the burgeoning pull to the terraces of professional soccer and the lure of rugby league's cash were to see many players at international and lower levels 'go north' and many fans turn to pastures new during the early 1920s.

Rhymney's 'pasture' included the old colliery spoil tip, and it was during the General Strike and its aftermath in 1926 that the jobless of the town flattened part of it to form, at the 'War Memorial Park', a cricket pitch. Many years later, it was to become the new ground of the town's rugby club.

Before that, however, in 1919 there remained in these islands that multitude of soldiers, seamen and airmen, British, New Zealanders, South Africans, Australians and Canadians, still in uniform, in good health, and not yet returned to their homes - in Britain or the other side of the world.

The 'Haka' in London

They included many fine rugby players. Good crowds were ready to watch British rugby talent, old and new, as well as those top performers from the Dominions who (as they were again to be in World War Two) were awaiting transport by sea. Many southern hemisphere players had their last-ever matches in Britain.

From these ranks sprang up many sides, with there often being three or four 'New Zealand' teams playing on the same day. Most notable of the New Zealand teams was the Army XV, who played Wales, for example, while the 'B' (Trench) team toured against clubs and counties. 'Trench' sides from New Zealand, Australia and South Africa, who had been playing each other (and French sides) across the Channel eventually arrived and played trials against their countrymen prior to the King's Cup.

There was a mixture of pre- and post-war internationals-in-waiting available, while in January, the Army decided to allow rugby league players to play union until the end of the 1918-19 season – as long as they played for Army sides only. The Welsh Rugby Union, however, originally decided that no league players would be allowed to play with union players in Wales. They were suspicious that several of the New Zealand side had played professional rugby before the war and wanted a guarantee that they were all amateurs.

Not all agreed, one British officer responding: *"As if it matters a damn whether they are amateurs or professionals when they have come to this country to fight and die for us."* The WRU realised they had misjudged the public sentiment, dropped their complaint and did not raise the issue again.

So the stage was set for the return to some high-quality rugby (or 'rugger', as it had always been in England). No international matches were played in 1918, but after the Armistice, many more games were played in what would have been the 1918-1919 season, culminating, as we shall see, in the King's Cup competition between those Forces' contingents from the corners of the globe.

(In 1998 I was pleased to aid Air Commodore John Mace as he wrote his wonderful 'History of the Royal Air Force 1919-1999', and I loved the words he quoted about Services rugby players: *"It is often said that the Army is full of gentlemen trying to be professionals, while the Royal Navy is full of professionals trying to be gentlemen and the Royal Air Force is full of neither, trying to be both!"*)

Not all in the Army managed to be gentlemen, it seems. As the ban on games was lifted (the WRU, for instance, doing so on November 27), Mr A J Trollope, Hon Secretary and Treasurer of the London Society of Referees, was immediately moved to report: *"My committee, in consequence of the very undesirable character of recent matches in which the Welsh Guards have participated, have decided in future to refuse to appoint a referee for any game in which the Guards are engaged. They feel they are acting in the best interests of Rugby Football by refusing to countenance these exhibitions of foul play, which can only bring discredit on the game."* The side was disbanded as a result – and these were the 'good old days, eh?!

On November 30, Yorkshire were playing the Northern Command at Leeds for military charities, a week later the NZ HQ Staff thrashed the United Services at Portsmouth 52-0 with 14 tries, seven of them by centre W L Henry of the Canterbury Infantry Regiment.

It was closer at Richmond on December 13, with the South African Services edging out their Canadian Services counterparts 9-0, but the New Zealand Services were clearly too good for the Public School Services in a 16-0 win at the same venue on December 21. The Public School side

Pill Harriers Patriotic Invincible Rugby Football Team 1918-19, including Jack Whitfield, Walter Martin and every-inch-the-boxer Jerry Shea

included B Melbourne G Thomas at centre, but it was as a wing that he was to win a Wales cap in 1919.

As the Christmas by which the war would be over, finally arrived, Boxing Day 1918 saw a host of games. Leicester's first match in three and a half years saw them beat the 4th Leicestershire Regiment 6-5 at Welford Road, wing Percy William Lawrie (two caps for England 1910-11) scoring both Leicester tries.

A comparative feast of festive rugby in Wales found a New Zealand XV narrowly getting past Cardiff 8-6 at the Arms Park, on the same day as the big Wales-NZ Services encounter in Swansea. Meanwhile the Newport Docks-based side, Pill Harriers, reputedly unbeaten during the war with plenty of to-ing and fro-ing of Newport players, and certainly invincible 1918-19, started a three wins in three days sequence.

At Rodney Parade, Newport, they saw off the Australian Headquarters Staff Battalion 12-3, then the New Zealand Services, 13-0. Pill tries came from Jerry Shea (capped by Wales 1919-21), Tom Jones and Steve Roberts, Cheshire dropping a goal. Finally, the Monmouthshire Regiment went under 31-0 for a memorable hat-trick even by the standards of the club which also produced the father and son duo, George 'Twyber' and William 'Bunner' Travers, for Wales.

The Australian HQ Staff suffered again, 12-0 at Cardiff two days later, in between perhaps the most significant pair of post-war clashes to that point: between a Wales XV and the New Zealand Expeditionary Force, who met in a non-cap game at Swansea on Boxing Day and again six days later on New Year's Day, 1919 in Cardiff, Field-Marshal Sir Douglas Haig granting leave to play for ten of the Wales side.

There was action continuing in France, too, but this time on the rugby field, with New Year's Day finding France downing a Wales XV, probably the 38th Welsh Division side, 13-6 in Paris. They scored three tries and two conversions to two tries. Four days later a measure of revenge was extracted when the Welsh XV beat Paris 9-6.

Meanwhile, something nearer a real Welsh side had twice been in action on home soil:

Travers, junior and senior

December 26, 1918 – Wales XV 3 New Zealand Services 0
St. Helen's, Swansea – Attendance 20,000

A strong New Zealand 'Trench' team had been touring, but none of those players were available, arriving just too late to play. Instead, the New Zealand authorities got together players from various camps in Britain and put out what they called 'a weakened team', hoping to strengthen it in the return match six days later.

The visitors had played just five days earlier in that win over the Public Schools Services, but eight of this supposedly 'below-strength' side had already been capped for their country, with three others gaining full honours later.

They gave a splendid account of themselves, as before a crowd of 20,000, play was fast and furious. There was no score in the first half. Then, Evan Davies and Reg Plummer worked wing Jim Bacon in at the corner for the only points.

The first real stoppage was after 65 minutes when Charles Brown of New Zealand was knocked out, but he soon resumed, as did Sid Jerram, who played superbly for Wales.

Sid Jerram

Rugby league players, like him, had been allowed to play and Wales included six pre-war caps and four who gained them later: five, if the 'Huddlestone' named in the pack by the press was in fact Dai Hiddlestone, as seems thoroughly likely.

So, this was a quality encounter with up to 22 of the 30 players on show past or future internationals: a pointer, too, to how many of the rugby players of the day from home and abroad had joined up, or been called up, for action in the war.

While, understandably, no caps were awarded for this game, the Welsh public will no doubt have been thrilled to see the final score exactly reflect that most famous of tallies, the single winger's-try, 3-0 win over the 'Originals', the NZ All Black tourists of 1905.

WALES XV – J L G Thomas (Neath); *R C S Plummer (Newport), *W A Davies (Leeds RL), +E Davies (Maesteg), J A Bacon (Leeds RL); +B Beynon (Swansea), S G Jerram (Wigan RL); *T J Lloyd (Neath), *A P

Coldrick (Wigan RL), +D D Hiddlestone (Hendy); *T Williams (Swansea), *W J Jenkins (Cardiff), +E T Parker (Swansea), +J Jones (Swansea/Aberavon), M Lloyd (Neath).

Try – J Bacon.

NEW ZEALAND SERVICES – *J G O'Brien; +P W Storey, *E A P Cockcroft, *R W Roberts; G J McNaught, P Tureia; *C Brown; *H V Murray, *E W Hasell, R Sellars, *N A Wilson, +J E Moffitt, *J A Bruce, +R Fogarty, J Kissick.

(* – denotes capped before the war; + – capped after the war; RL – rugby league)

Referee – Mr Frank W Best (Penarth). (NB: He was my wife's grandfather's brother and one of three rugby-playing brothers from Penarth).

The sides then met in a return game in Cardiff, just six days after their Boxing Day encounter at Swansea.

January 1, 1919 – Wales XV 3 New Zealand Services 3
Arms Park, Cardiff – Attendance 10,000

The New Zealand team was again picked from those already stationed and playing in Britain, as their Trench team, which had played many games across the Channel, could not yet be used. Wales saw three chosen forwards drop out and made 12 changes, retaining only wings Reg Plummer and Jim Bacon plus Percy Coldrick in the pack. Pre-war cap Clem Lewis came in at fly half.

New Zealand made only two changes with Jack Stohr and Arthur Singe replacing Parekura Tureai and Toby Murray. The match was played in torrents of rain and the pitch was said to be 'as muddy as a Flanders battlefield!'

Wales scored first when Johnny Coughlin picked up a loose ball, sending it to Reg Plummer, who kicked ahead and Coughlin, following up, won the race to the line.

New Zealand levelled in the second half when Charles Brown passed to Jack McNaught, who in turn put Richard Roberts in for the try. Wales almost snatched the win, but Eric Cockcroft just got back to save and the game ended almost in the dark.

A New Zealand report stated: "It was a brilliant exhibition under wretched conditions and it was a tribute to the enthusiasm of Welsh Rugby devotees that 10,000 of them turned out on such a day.

"It was certain that Wales could not have fielded a more versatile or better-balanced back division, while the New Zealand forwards were at least equal to the pack captained by Dave Gallaher in the ever-memorable game of 13 years ago when the All Blacks lost the only match of their tour by one try.

"Melbourne Thomas, the St Bart's student, who made his debut in top-class football, was in brilliant form at centre, and his international cap is waiting for him."

WALES XV – D Williams; *R C S Plummer, +B M G Thomas, J Coughlin, J A Bacon (RL); *+J C M Lewis, *R A Lloyd (RL); J Webb, *A P Coldrick (RL), D Llewellyn, T Davies, G Samuels, C Pavey, P C Hammans, W C Jones.

Try – Coughlin.

NEW ZEALAND SERVICES – *J G O'Brien; *L B Stohr, *E R W Roberts, +P W Storey; G J McNaught, *E A P Cockcroft; *C Brown; R Sellars, *E W Hasell, +J E Moffitt, *N A Wilson, *J A Bruce, J Kissick, +R Fogarty, A P Singe.

Try – Roberts.

Referee – Not known.

The men who represented the Wales XV in the first match were:

J L GWYN THOMAS
Full back. Born 14/3/1891. Wales U-16 (1905)/Neath/Barbarians. Neath's first Barbarian (1912), a fine cricketer, son of a Mayor of Neath. Edinburgh Univ. Capt. in Northumberland Fusiliers, wounded WW1, captained Neath in 1920-21. Welsh reserve 1921. Died 10/4/1932 at 41.

Reginald (Reg) Clifford Stanley PLUMMER
Wing. Born Newport 29/12/1888. Died Newport 18/6/1953. Long Ashton School, Bristol/Newport (132 tries in 287 games)/London Welsh/

Barbarians. He toured with GB to South Africa in 1910 (12 games, 6 tries). 5 caps (1912-13). Brother-in-law of Tommy Vile. Corporal in the Royal Engineers. Hotelier.

William Avon (Willie) DAVIES

Centre. Born Aberavon 27/12/1890. Died Exeter 18/9/1967. Aberavon Council School/Pt Talbot Council School/Exeter University/Aberavon/ Swansea/Plymouth/ Devon Albion/Devon/Glamorgan County. 2 caps (1912). Schoolmaster. Rugby league for Leeds (from 1913, 278 games, 77 tries, 28 goals)/ Wales RL (2 caps)/Other Nationalities (1 cap)/GB (2 caps). He was a Warrant Schoolmaster in the Navy on the flagship of Admiral Sir H E Thomas.

Willie Davies

Evan (Ianto) Davies

Centre. Born Maesteg c.1893. Died Maesteg 10/9/1945. Plasnewydd School, Maesteg/Maesteg Rovers/Maesteg (captain 1920-21)/Llanelli/London Welsh/Glamorgan County. 1 cap (1919 as full back). Royal Field Artillery and Welch Regiment. Collier.

James Arthur (Jim) BACON

Wing. Born Wattsville 10/9/1896. Death date not known. Cross Keys. Rugby league for Leeds (from January 1919, 276 games and 121 tries)/ Wales RL (6 caps)/GB (11 caps inc 1920 tour). Coached Castleford RL (1928-29). Married in Bramley 1927. Played for Leeds under the name of Arthur James in 1918! He played in the Leeds winning RL Cup Final team of 1923.

Benjamin (Ben) BEYNON

Fly half. Born Swansea 14/3/1894. Died Swansea 21/5/1969. Manselton/Swansea. 2 caps (1920). Tin Worker/Docker/Painter & Decorator. Rugby league for Oldham (94

Jim Bacon, in Rugby League colours

games) and played in 1925 RL Cup final win. Played professional soccer for Swansea Town, including scoring the goal that knocked Blackburn Rovers out of the 1915 FA Cup.

Sidney George (Sid) JERRAM
Scrum half. Born Swansea April-June 1891. Died Swansea c.1959. Swansea (played in their 3-0 win over South Africa in 1912). Married in Swansea 1915. Rugby league for Wigan (from 1914, 245 games, 202 points)/Wales RL (5 caps)/Other Nationalities (1 cap), played in Wigan's RL Cup Final win of 1924.

Thomas John (TC) LLOYD
Forward. Born Neath Oct-Dec 1882. Died Neath 27/4/1938. 7 caps (1909-14). Glynneath School/Glynneath (captain 1903-04)/Neath (captain 1913-14). Collier, then Bookmaker. Played for Neath v South Africa in 1912 and for Wales in the non-cap match against the Barbarians in 1915. He also appeared against Australia in 1908 for both Glamorgan County and the combined Neath/Aberavon side. Brother of 'Mogs' Lloyd who played in this 1918 match.

Albert Percival (Percy) COLDRICK
Forward. Born Oct-Dec Llangattock Juxta Caerleon c.1888. Died Wigan 26/12/1953. Crumlin/Newport (97games)/Weston/Talywain/Pontypool Monmouthshire. 6 caps (1911-12). Rugby league for Wigan (280 games, 1912-24, 79 tries)/St Helen's (17 games, 1925-26)/Wales RL (2 caps)/GB (3 caps on their 1914 tour). Was a foreman railway platelayer.

Percy Coldrick

David Daniel (Dai) HIDDLESTONE
Forward. Listed as 'Huddlestone of Newport', but seemingly this was Dai Hiddlestone of Hendy. 5 caps (1922-24). Born Hendy 14/6/1890. Died Hendy 16/11/1973. Hendy/Llanelli (captain 1919-20)/Neath (captain 1924-25). Won his caps from Neath – the last at the age of 34. Worked at Morlais Colliery/Gorseinon tinplate works as a bar cutter. On Crawshay's

Welsh committee and refereed combined Aberavon/Neath v New Zealand in 1935. His grandson was Terry Price (8 caps, 1965-67).

Thomas (Tom) WILLIAMS
Forward. Born Dunvant c.1887. Died Swansea 13/8/1927 (aged 39). Swansea (played centre v South Africa 1912). 6 caps (1912-14). Captain in the Royal Engineers. Worked for Gower Rural District Council (1925-27). Dropped out of Wales XV v Barbarians 1915 through injury.

William Joseph (Billy) JENKINS
Forward. Born Cardiff April-June 1885. Died Cardiff 23/12/1956. Played for Canton in west Cardiff and then Cardiff (158 games, 1909-10 to 1919-20, 19 tries). Corporal in the Royal West Kent Regiment in WW1. Played for Cardiff against South Africa 1912 and for Wales XV v Barbarians 1915. 4 caps (1912-13). A builder. His brother, Eddie, played soccer for Wales.

Billy Jenkins

Edwin Thomas (Tom) PARKER
Forward. Born Llansamlet, near Swansea 29/3/1891. Died Tredegar 25/11/1967. 15 caps (1919-23). Captained Wales seven times, unbeaten in them with six wins and a draw. Llansamlet School/Swansea. Tinplate worker then a picker in Ebbw Vale Stelworks. His brother, Dai, won ten caps (1924-30) and toured with the British team to NZ in 1930.

James (Jim) JONES
Forward. Born first quarter of 1894 in Blaengwynfi. Died Briton Ferry 3/3/1934. Cymmer/Swansea (one cap in 1919)/Aberavon (in his last five caps, club captain 1921-23) 6 caps (1919-21). Miner, then publican. He was badly injured against Scotland in 1920 and eventually retired

Jim Jones

with his hands paralysed due to a spinal injury from rugby. Known as 'Gentleman Jim', he became publican of the Royal Oak Hotel in Briton Ferry, but was only 40 when he died of pneumonia and left a wife and two children. His cap and jerseys have been lost, possibly in an Aberavon RFC fire.

Morgan (Mogs) LLOYD
Forward. Neath. Brother of 'TC' Lloyd (7 caps, 1909-1914), who also played in this match.

Those who only appeared for the Wales XV in the second of the games were:

David (Dai) WILLIAMS
Full back. Swansea (played against South Africa 1912)/Newport.

Johnny COUGHLIN
Centre. Cardiff (20 games, 1919-20 to 1920-21). Sent off against Newport 19/12/1919.

Robert A (Bobby) LLOYD
Scrum half. Born Crickhowell c.1888. Died Halifax 18/1/1930. Pontypool/ Hafodyrynys (captain 1913-14). A collier, then a publican. 7 caps (1913-14). Joined Halifax rugby league in 1914 and played for Wales RL and GB, including the tour to Australia in 1920. Played for Monmouthshire vs South Africa 1912. Dubbed 'The Hafodyrynys Wonder'.

David (Dai) LLEWELLYN
Forward. Cardiff (103 games, 1913-14 until 1923-24).

G SAMUELS
Forward. Cardiff (5 games, 1919-20).

The other five forwards were relatively unknown: – **C Pavey** (Penarth); **Jack Webb** (Abertillery); **Tom Davies** (Pontypool); **P C Hammans** (Swansea) and **W C Jones** (Welch Regiment).

Hammans may have been **Harry Hiams** (Swansea), who won two caps in 1912. (He also played for Llanelli/Aberavon/London Welsh. Served as a Sergeant in Royal Garrison (Field) Artillery and later worked for ICI at Landore. Played for Llanelli and Glamorgan vs South Africa 1912. Born c.1886. Died Swansea 10/4/1954.

Plummer, Bacon and Coldrick have been detailed in the Boxing Day 1918 match, Thomas in the April 1919 international found later in the book and Lewis in the King's Cup, when playing for the Mother Country.

For the New Zealand Services XV:

Details of eleven members of the team can be found in the later chapters on the King's Cup, but the following players, who featured in one or both of these Wales XV clashes, did not appear in that competition:

Eric Arthur Percy COCKCROFT
Centre (also Full back). Born Clinton 10/9/1890. Died Ashburton 2/4/1973. Southland Boys High School/University Club of Otago/ Otago/ Pirates RFC/South Canterbury/Mataura/Timaru HSOB/South Island. 3 caps (1913-14). Nephew of Samuel George Cockcroft (All Black 1893-94). New Zealand Bowls international. Headmaster. Lieutenant, Canterbury Infantry Regiment.

Parekura TUREIA
Five-eighth. Served with Pioneers. Was not allowed to go on the tour to South Africa in 1919 as he was a Maori.

Harold Vivian (Toby) MURRAY
Forward. Born Christchurch 9/2/1888. Died Amberley 4/7/1971. Christ's College/Irwell RFC/Springfield RFC/Canterbury/South Island. 4 caps (1913-14). Corporal in the Army, Machine Gun Corps. Farmer/sheep breeder and member of the Electric Power Board.

John Alexander (Alex) BRUCE
Forward. Did not play in the King's Cup but his details can be found later, in the section on the 1919 tour to South Africa.

The day after the second match, a Welsh civilian death occurred to add one more to the list of the lost: but this time it was not through war that Wales mourned the passing, all too young, of their, and perhaps the world's, first rugby superstar.

Monkey' Gould

On January 2, Joseph Arthur 'Monkey' Gould (known as A J Gould), winner of 27 caps 1885-1897, 'The Prince of Threequarters', died in his native Newport of a severe internal haemorrhage, aged 54. Two of his brothers also played for Wales: Robert (11 caps 1882-87) and George Herbert (Bert) (3 caps 1892-93).

Arthur was a public works contractor, then a representative and cashier for Phillips Brewery. The 'testimonial' presentation to him of the deeds of a house had caused huge controversy between Wales and the International Rugby Board. Fittingly, the burial was officiated by the Rev Alfred Augustus Matthews, who had won his Welsh cap in 1886.

Meanwhile, the pace of rugby's resumption was clearly picking up, especially with those 'Trench' teams of the various nations arriving back from France and staging trials and representative games. Several of their players were to stay on in Britain to attend medical colleges and universities.

Incidentally, on February 26, Oxford University had their first match in five years when they defeated Guy's Hospital 9-6, while Llanelli's first official game after the war on January 25, had seen a 3-0 win over a NZ Army XV (from the Larkhill Garrison in Wiltshire) at Stradey Park.

Some clubs found it harder to get a strong side quickly back on the field than others, as suggested when Pill Harriers, with 15 tries and six conversions, beat Bristol 57-3 on January 18. Further afield, meanwhile, although thousands of troops had been shipped to Britain, very many were still at a variety of far-flung theatres of war. They, too, had their sport.

Major Sydney Albert Middleton, DSO, of the 19th Battalion, Australian Imperial Services had been appointed to organise several sports, with matches in Inter-Battalion, Inter-Brigade and Corps competitions in France, Belgium, England and the Middle East. Some 60-70 Australian rugby players were brought to Paris, and on January 19th those chosen from them defeated the French Army by 3-0 (one try), before a crowd of some 20,000.

Australia then had two weeks training in Belgium before travelling to England. Jimmy Clarken and Munro ('Money') Fraser did the coaching, while W F (Wally) Matthews was the manager.

The game had been hailed by the French papers as an international, but no caps were awarded. The press often tagged 'trial' games internationals, too, but in truth the only match where caps were awarded was to be when Wales met the New Zealand Services team at Cardiff Arms Park in April, in a match detailed later.

Major Middleton had an amazing sporting career, having played rugby for Glebe and NSW (against the GB team of 1908) and toured with Australia to GB and North America in 1908-09. He was sent off against Oxford University for punching but won a test spot against England.

He played in their Olympic rugby win of 1908 and as captain in three more tests against New Zealand in 1910. He then turned to rowing, was in the Australian eight that rowed in the 1912 Stockholm Olympics and the winning eight at the Henley Regatta in 1920. He died in Kensington, London in 1945 aged 63.

Sydney Middleton (ARU, via ESPN website)

Other news from France was that, although the Versailles negotiations were making slow progress, at least one argument had been settled: but on the rugby front. On February 4, came the news from the French capital that Scotland and France had ended the six-year-long dispute that had begun with crowd trouble on the Paris pitch in 1913.

Amongst the growing gamut of games the preparations for the King's Cup loomed large, and will be dealt with at length in the next section. However, it seems appropriate to highlight two in particular of the contests in 1918-19 outside that competition.

The first is a match that took place while the King's Cup was going on, when, despite New Zealand playing Canada in the Cup on the same day, they fielded their strongest side against the potentially-stronger opposition of Yorkshire. They proved far too good for their hosts, scoring 11 tries, as the new Bradford RFC ground was opened by the Lord Mayor of Bradford.

The programme, priced at two pence and showing a 3.30pm kick-off, reported: *"The club was formed to revive in Bradford the popular pastime of Rugby Football. The ground at Lidget Green was acquired in May, 1914 and the amount so far laid out was four thousand pounds."*

Programme Cover for Yorkshire v NZ 1919

Yorkshire Team	New Zealand Team
BACK—	**BACK—**
1 Capt. A. Marshall	1 F. O. Brion
THREE-QUARTER BACKS—	**THREE-QUARTER BACKS—**
2 E. Haselwere	2 P. Storey
3 Lieut. E. McNaught, M.C.	3 J. Stohr
4 Capt. E. Myers, M.C.	4 J. Ford
5 Capt. S. P. S. Kitching	**FIVE-EIGHTHS—**
	5 J. McNaught
HALF-BACKS—	6 W. Fea
6 Bombr. A. King	**HALF-BACK —**
7 Lieut. A. S. Hamilton	7 C. Brown
	FORWARDS—
FORWARDS—	8 E. Hazell
8 Capt. J. H. Eddison, M.C. Capt.	9 R. Sellars
9 J. Allen	10 J. Kissick
10 C. Tosney	11 L. Cockroft
11 F. Trenham	12 A. Wilson
12 Lieut. C. A. Stockdale	13 M. Belliss
13 Capt. P. Walker	14 J. West
14 Lieut. H. J. White	**WING FORWARD—**
15 Capt. J. Woolley	15 A. Singe

Referee - A. E. N. YEADON.

The teams page

March 8, 1919 – Yorkshire 5 New Zealand Services 41
Lidget Green, Bradford – Attendance 10,000

Yorkshire –D V D Marshall; E E Haselmere, E E Myers, E McNaught, G P S Kitching; A S Hamilton, A King; J H Eddison, W J Allen, F Trentham, H J White, C Tosney, C A Stockdale, P Walker, J Woolley.

Try – Haselmere. **Con**: King.

New Zealand Services – J G O'Brien; W A Ford, L B Stohr, P W Storey; G J McNaught, W R Fea; C Brown; A P Singe, E W Hasell, R Sellars, N A Wilson, A H West, E A Belliss, J Kissick, E L J Cockroft.

Tries – Fea 3, Stohr 3, Storey 2, Ford 2, Kissick. **Cons** – Stohr 4.

Referee – Mr A E N Yeadon, a former Yorkshire County forward.

Yorkshire v New Zealand Services XV, Bradford, 1919

Back Row (left to right)—P. WALKER, Ilkley; Capt. J. WOOLLEY, Blackheath and Rest of England; H. J. WHITE, Headingley; Lt. G J. McNAUGHT; E. W. HASELL, R. SELLARS; P. TURRAI; E. WATKINS, *Trainer*; M. P. NAUGHTON, *Hon. Sec. Middle Row*—A. E. N. YEADON, *Referee*; V. DIXON-MARSHALL, Headingley; E. McNAUGHT, Clydesdale; J. P. S. KITCHING, Dragoon Guards; J. ALLEN, Leicester; C. A. STOCKDALE, Headingley; C. TOSNEY, Skipton; J. KISSICK; A. WEST; A. SINGE; Lt. SANDS; P. ALLEN; J. DOUGLAS; A. SMITH; A. BRUCE. *Front Row (seated)*—R. F. OAKES, *Hon. Sec. Y.R.F.C.*; E. MYERS, Headingley and Rest of England; A. S. HAMILTON, Headingley and Scotland; F. TRENHAM; Otley and North of England; J. H. EDDISON (*Capt.*), Headingley and England; The Right Hon. The Lord Mayor of Leeds, JOSEPH HENRY, Esq.; Lt.-Col. J. L. HICKSON, *President Y.R.F.U.*; The Right Hon. The Lord Mayor of Bradford, Ald. A. HAYHURST; A. WILSON (*Capt.*); W. R. FEA; P. STOREY; W. FORD; L. COCKROFT; E. BELLIS; J. STOHR; Capt. A. DEAN (*Manager*). *Sat on Ground*—A. KING, Headingley and North of England; E. HASELMERE, Leicester; C. BROWN; J. O'BRIEN.

The sides for that 8th March clash

Yorkshire included centres Lt. E McNaught and Capt. Eddie Myers, forward Capt. Philip Walker and skipper, Capt. John Eddison, who had all been awarded the MC. New Zealand also had a McNaught in their backs, but all the home hopes came to nought, as the cartoonist of the day stressed the vistors' quality: *'the best to have been seen there since the All Blacks of 1905-6'.* The 10,000 crowd were most impressed, too.

"ALL BLACKS" AS MASTERS OF THE RUGBY GAME.

The New Zealand team, which beat Yorkshire on Saturday at the opening of the new ground of the Bradford Rugby Club, is regarded as the best all-round Colonial side seen in England since the famous All Blacks were here in 1905-6. The attendance of 10,000 was the largest recorded at a handling game in Bradford since the Association code invaded the city.

Yorkshire's representatives were: -

John Horncastle EDDISON, MC (captain)
England 4 caps, forward (1912). Born Edinburgh 25/8/1888. Died Edinburgh 18/11/1982 aged 94. Ilkley Grammar School/Bromsgrove School/Headingley/Barbarians. Played for North of England v South Africa 1912. A Captain/Lieutenant in the Royal Field Artillery, he became a major in the West Riding Brigade, being mentioned in despatches, then an official in the North British Mercantile Insurance Company 1907-1951. He became a referee.

Captain D V DIXON-MARSHALL
Full back. Leeds University/Headingley.

Edward Ernest (Teddy) HASELMERE
Born Rugby 1/4/1895. Died Rugby 8/10/1983. Wing. One of the most prolific try-scorers and fastest wings in England. Rugby/Leicester/Northampton/England Trials/Leicestershire/Warwickshire. Became a referee. Engineer with British Thomson-Houston of Rugby.

Edward (Eddie) MYERS, MC
England 18 caps, centre/fly half (1920-25). Dollar Academy/Leeds University/Headingley/Leicester/Bradford. Born in New York (USA) 23/9/1895. Died Bradford 29/3/1956. Born of Yorkshire parents in the USA, schooled in Scotland, becoming a director of a textile company. Captain in the West Yorkshire Regiment and was wounded three times. He skippered Yorkshire v the New Zealand tourists of 1924-5.

E McNAUGHT, MC
Centre. Clydesdale RFC. Lieutenant in Army.

G P S KITCHING
Wing. Pickering RFC. Lieut. then Captain, Inniskilling Dragoons.

Eddie Myers went on to win 18 England Caps

Andrew Steven HAMILTON
Scotland 2 caps, fly half and centre (1914-1920). Born Hamilton 8/3/1893. Died Leeds 3/11/1975. Ripon Grammar School/Headingley/ Barbarians. Played for North of England v South Africa 1912. Lieutenant in the 15th West Yorkshire Regiment. Civil Engineer.

A KING
Scrum half. Headingley. Played for North of England v South Africa in 1912. Bombardier.

Walter James (Jimmy, Jumbo) ALLEN
Forward. Born Rugby c 1882. Died Warwick c 1953. Leicester/England Trial/Midland Counties. Captain in Army. Mechanic.

F TRENTHAM
Forward. Otley/Barbarians.

H J WHITE
Forward. Headingley/Bradford/Barbarians. Lieutenant in Army.

C TOSNEY
Forward. Skipton RFC (captain 1910-12)/Yorkshire (31 apps, 1908-19).

C A STOCKDALE
Forward. Headingley RFC. Lieutenant in Royal Field Artillery.

Philip H C WALKER, MC and Bar.
Forward. Ilkley RFC/Oxford RFC. Army Capt. Mentioned in despatches.

J WOOLLEY
Forward. Birkenhead RFC/Blackheath. Captain in Army.

A week later the New Zealanders faced another major challenge, but outside of the ongoing King's Cup fixtures. An England XV, awarded no caps but with seven past or future internationals in the ranks, put up stronger resistance at Leicester, who supplied nine of the home side.

March 15, 1919 – England XV 3 New Zealand Services 11
Welford Rd, Leicester

England XV – D Williams (club not known, but possibly Swansea); +Edward Myers, MC (Leicester/West Yorkshire Regiment), Lionel Hamblin (Gloucester/Royal Berkshire and Gloucestershire Regiments), *Willie Watts (Leicester), Edward E Haselmere (Leicester/Yorkshire); A King (Yorkshire), *George William ('Pedlar') Wood (Leicester); Alfred Bates (Leicester), *George Ward (Leicester), +Frank Taylor (Leicester/Leicestershire Regiment), *Dr Arthur Gilbert Bull (Northampton/Army), Frank K Gaccon (Cardiff), Gordon Vears (Leicester), +George F Holford (Gloucester/Manchester Regiment), D J Ferguson (Leicester).

Try – Gaccon.

New Zealand Services – *J G O'Brien; +W A Ford, *L B Stohr, +P W Storey; G J McNaught, +W R Fea; *C Brown (capt); *N A Wilson, *E W Hasell, R Sellars, E L J Cockcroft, J Kissick, +E A Belliss, P Gilchrist, +A H West.

Tries – Fea, Ford. **Con –** Stohr. **Pen –** Stohr.

Referee – Not known.

However, the visitors were fielding what was close to their best outfit, for only Alf West had not previously appeared in this 'first' team. That proved more than enough, and a pair of tries by five-eighth Billy Fea and swift wing 'Jockey' Ford, one improved by Stohr, who also landed a penalty, outweighed England's single try by Cardiff's Frank Gaccon.

A further boost to morale, if such were needed, then, before the 'Men in Black' returned to the tournament proper. Meanwhile the weekly – and often midweek – swing of rugby went on, and details of the rest of the season at levels below the King's Cup can be found in the Appendix.

3

The King's Cup

'The side is being carefully chosen from thousands of available men'

On January 13, 1919, at a general meeting of the Army RU, held at the Library of the Horse Guards in Whitehall, London, and presided over by Colonel C G Liddell, CMG, DSO, it was decided that a rugby tournament should be played in March and April between New Zealand, South Africa, Australia, Canada, the newly-formed Royal Air Force and the 'Mother Country'.

In reality, Mother Country (also sometimes labelled the Home Countries) was the British Army; Canada was the Canadian Expeditionary Force; New Zealand was the New Zealand Army; South Africa was the South African Forces and Australia was the Australian Imperial Forces. The Royal Navy felt unable to raise a fully-representative XV. Rugby league players in the Army, RAF and Royal Navy were allowed to take part in union games until the end of the season.

Note that it was not named the King's Cup at this stage: the competition was initially called The Imperial Services Tournament. No caps were to be awarded in the 15 matches to be played, after which the winners would play against France in a challenge match. Two points were to be awarded for a win and one for a draw, though in the event there were no drawn matches.

The round-robin format of this 'proto-World Cup' meant that a play-off was eventually necessary, both New Zealand and the Mother Country winning four and losing one of their five matches.

Canada, less steeped in rugby tradition and touring history than the other Dominions, was likely to find the tournament a real challenge, while one of the other competitors was to be a youthful organization indeed – not yet 12 months old.

On April 1, 1918, The Royal Air Force had been formed from an amalgamation of the Royal Naval Air Service and the Royal Flying Corps,

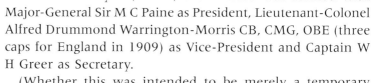

THE CANADIAN TEAM OF FOOTBALLERS NOW ON TOUR IN ENGLAND

The names, reading from left to right, are : Back row—R. H. Britten, E. M. Phillips; second row—S. S. Dumoulin, N. C. Ogilvie, C. MacDonald, H. Fenarty, O. Ravdle; third row—J. P. Craig, S. Bauld, C. W. Darling, J. W. S. MacClure (captain), J. Powers, K. Scholfield, J. Purvis, W. R. Marshall; front row— A. Gillespie, G. W. W. Farrell, A. Clifford Jack

The Canadian tourists of 1902

and according to *The Times,* the RAF Rugby Union was only formed a day after the tournament was formulated.

It reported that on January 14, 1919, the RAFRU was formed with Major-General Sir M C Paine as President, Lieutenant-Colonel Alfred Drummond Warrington-Morris CB, CMG, OBE (three caps for England in 1909) as Vice-President and Captain W H Greer as Secretary.

(Whether this was intended to be merely a temporary arrangement is unclear, but John Mace in his *History of Royal Air Force Rugby* dates the establishment of the RAFRU from a year later, at the meeting of January 15, 1920. William Wavell 'Wakers' Wakefield was to be both Secretary and Captain, and later lead Cambridge and England, while 'WM' (Warrington-Morris) was still on the Committee at his passing, 42 years later).

New the organisation might be, but amongst the potential players for the 'Junior' Service were experienced and talented performers, of whom 'Wakers' would soon be pre-eminent:

12. W. W. WAKEFIELD

W W 'Wakers' Wakefield

and that sort of quality would be crucial to the credibility and the lasting legacy of this first 'world gathering' of rugby talent.

Significantly, a report in the *Taranaki Daily News* of February 1919 helps underline two of the points made in these chapters: the varied and often less-than-sparkling nature of some of the sides billed as 'All Blacks' during and just after the war, and by contrast the top quality and major importance of the New Zealand side (and several others) which would be playing in what became the King's Cup proper. To quote that NZ daily:

....'*People who have read brief, unsatisfactory cabled reports of matches between "All Blacks" and English and Welsh teams may have an impression that merely "scratch sides" have represented New Zealand. A Welsh paper remarked before the match at Swansea on Boxing Day: "The mistake should not be made of thinking that this is just one of the ordinary All Black teams which so frequently play second-rate clubs in the Principality, for such an idea would be entirely erroneous. The side coming to Swansea is being carefully chosen from many thousands of available men in France, and will play a series of games in France so as to get used to one another's methods. The Colonials make no secret of the fact that their team will, without a shadow of doubt, be one of the most formidable sides which has ever toured. The players are being specially reserved for international matches only, and will not arrange any fixtures, unless against representative, national fifteens". The plain truth is that this touring team is under the management of the N.Z.E.F. Sport Control Board, of which the secretary is Regimental Staff-Sergeant M.P. Naughton, of Wellington. In a letter to a relative in Wellington, Sgt. Naughton states: "On an average I send and receive about fifty telegrams a day, and have special reporters from all the London papers waiting on me daily. The papers over here call us wonderful people, and one paper had myself as the 'secretary on wires.' We are playing All Wales at Swansea on Boxing Day (you will see the report of it in the cables) and also at Cardiff on New Year's Day. They expect 60,000 people present, and the whole show is to be kinematographed; so you will see it all later on. Then we play the Midland Counties at Leicester, and later play in Glasgow and Edinburgh, and after that at Dublin and Cork. Then we go over and play one match in Paris and one on the Rhine. Then follows one in Rome. After coming home we play Devon at Devonport, All Wales again on Easter Monday at Swansea, and finally wind up by playing the biggest game in the history of Rugby against an All British team, composed of all internationals from England, Scotland, Wales, and Ireland, for which I have to arrange guarantees to the extent of close on £1250. I have also to arrange Association football, hockey, boxing, and cross-country matches for the whole New Zealand Expeditionary Force; and every month I have to make a report to the War Office, London".... '*

The chronology of the matches was to change a little, but the scale of the plan was certainly adhered to – plus a tour of South Africa on the way home! Clearly, this New Zealand side was to be, in effect, 'the real thing': as that Taranaki report's heading stressed, "All Blacks Again!" Every effort was made to ensure that outcome, as the returnees from France joined those who had been training or convalescing in Britain in trials and warm-up games prior to selection for the tournament.

One such was on January 18, as the New Zealand 'UK XV' took on the NZ Divisional Trench team (from France), losing a close thing 5-3 at Richmond. Used as a trial, the Trench team won it after wing 'Jockey' Ford cantered away from halfway, was tackled but found Belliss up in support to score, Stohr converting. The 'UK' team hit back as 'Ranji' Wilson was put clear for a try but Sellars hit a post with his conversion attempt.

In February both South Africa and The Army held trials at Queen's Club and Richmond, while Australia did so at Norbury, Chiswick and Gloucester. Meanwhile, after trials, the RAF took 25 players on a trip intending to play in Lille, Liege, Maubeuge, Cologne and Namur.

The party included as skipper winger Godfrey Maynard Wrentmore, a tourist with South Africa to GB in 1912 and the said W W (later Lord) Wakefield (England, 31 caps 1920-27). No games were played, though, due to frost and the players suffered poor conditions and accommodation (and much influenza) in a somewhat rash expedition which did not meet with much approval from 'Wakers'.

So it was not until February 26, 1919, that the RAF side played their first-ever game, losing 10-0 to the Royal Navy Depot, Devonport at Richmond. George Thom and Robert Simpson, later to be Scotland internationals, Wakefield, England's leader-in-waiting and the Wigan rugby league full back Billy Seddon all played, but in a 'combative' encounter Seddon received a kick to his head and followed the already-injured Thom from the field. One of the Naval forwards, Woods, was sent off.

The South African trials in England included 22-year-old forward Frank W Mellish, who was to win six caps with South Africa (1921-24). It is noteworthy, but far from unique in those times that he had first gained six caps for England (1920-21). (In keeping with those anomalies, it was also decided in February that South African players in the RAF could play for either the RAF or the South African Services as they wished. Several did in fact opt for the RAF).

Mellish, a colonel with the South African Heavy Artillery, was awarded the Military Cross in 1916. He fought in the South African Armoured Division in World War Two and later managed the 1951-52 South African team to GB and France. South Africa were also reinforced when the great forward, William Henry ('Boy') Morkel, a captain in World War One, who won nine caps between 1910-21, joined them.

The Richmond Athletic Ground was seeing plenty of action as the tournament's opening loomed. On February 20, New Zealand showed their paces in a 26-5 defeat of South Africa, two days after which the South African (UK) Services drew 6-all with the South African Trench team there. Four days on, given their full titles, those New Zealand Services beat the Australian Imperial Services 9-0 on those well used and picturesque south-west London acres.

The Australians had just beaten Leicester 8-6 at Welford Road, Wales' international centre Willie Watts making his Leicester debut, and on the day of the first King's Cup match, March 1, while the RAF and New Zealand were having their St David's Day clash at Swansea, the final Australian trial saw their Firsts down their Seconds 33-14 at Chiswick.

The Canadians, somewhat predictably, were finding it harder going. High scores were not the order of the day in the rugby of the time, so a 12-0 Chiswick defeat at the hands of New Zealand's Reserve XV on February 19, was not too promising.

They then lost 8-3 to St Bartholomew's Hospital at Wichmore Hill on February 22, and there was a bitter 'pill' indeed to swallow in Newport on March 1. The rampant Pill Harriers 'Invincibles' beat them 43-0: a pretty 'leeky' defence on St David's Day in the Principality!

On the same day the South Africans fine-tuned with a 14-3 win at Oxford University, who were themselves edged out 3-0 at home to the RAF four days later. (The students must have found travelling harder: when they went to Sandhurst a fortnight later and were swamped 48-0 by the Mother Country, the Army side had to loan Oxford five players).

With King George V, a regular visitor to Twickenham, putting his name and support to the competition, the preparations, successful or less-so, were close to complete: though several sides remained keen to get in regular match practice between the big tournament games, and also turned out reserve teams when possible to provide action for the squads – which were added to as players became available, and to which we can now turn.

George V, a Twickenham 'regular'

4

The Teams

"The players are being specially reserved for international matches only, and will not arrange any fixtures unless against representative, national fifteens"

Australia

Canada

France

Mother Country

New Zealand

RAF

South Africa

4.1   AUSTRALIA

While not possessed of the same fearsome and near-mythical reputation of their antipodean neighbours from New Zealand, Australia had over the previous 30 years developed and displayed a talent for skillful and successful sporting endeavour, mental and physical toughness, and pride in their projection of a young nation's capacity to compete in the world: not least in rugby union.

Not only rugby union either: and therein lay the potential rub. From quite early on the growth of rugby league, especially in Queensland as well as New South Wales, and – echoing the Canadian experience – an indigenous alternative in the Australian Rules football code so popular in Victoria, made the continued primacy of rugby union unlikely.

Nevertheless, enough talented young men still played the game and coveted the shirt of the 'Wallabies', rather than the rugby league 'Kangaroos' and the potential cash of the professional game, to make any representative Australian side a powerful proposition.

Moreover, the temporary 'amnesty' on league players in these particular circumstances of wartime and the King's Cup worked well for the Aussies, as well as for the All Blacks and the RAF.

So, there was some real strength in the 25 players who wore the Australian badge in the tournament, although the astonishing Dan Carroll – multi-national, multi-talented and Olympian in every sense – appeared only in their last two games.

Those players were:

Australian Imperial Forces Team. Who's the little boy?

In their first game, v the Mother Country:

Bruce McNeil (Jackie) BEITH Full back. Born Mudgee NSW 28/9/1893. Died September 1961. Barker College/Sydney University/Eastern Suburbs/NSW. 4 caps (1914-20). Captain in the RAMC/15th Field Ambulance/5th Infantry Battalion. Mentioned in dispatches. Stayed in England in 1920 to continue his studies. Dentist. Became a Queensland selector in 1933.

Dudley Colin (Dud) SUTTOR Wing. Born Koorowather, near Cowra, NSW 10/4/1892. Died Dee Why, NSW 15/4/1962. Shore School, Sydney/Bathurst/ NSW. 3 caps (1913). Sergeant 15th Company Australian Service Corps. Fruit grower. He died, aged 70, whilst competing in a 55 yard RSL swimming race at the Dee Why pool. He was a driver with the 15th Australian Army Service Corps. He saw service in Egypt, France and Belgium. Toured New Zealand in 1913. He married Betty Palmer in 1921 at Bathurst and lived at 'Myola', Tabrabucca, near Ilford before retiring to Edward Street, Dee Why in the 1950s and started a lawn mowing business. He was an excellent swimmer and surfer and had already won a 25-yard race on the day he died.

John Joseph (Darb, Jack) HICKEY Centre. Born Sydney 4/1/1887. Died Glebe, NSW 15/5/1950. Glebe RFC/Metropolian/NSW. Also played Rugby League for Glebe and Balmain and won cap for Australia. Corporal in the 56th NSW Battalion. Butcher. 2 caps (1908-09). Olympic Rugby gold medallist in 1908. He played Rugby League both pre and post-war. Allegedly threw his war medals into Sydney Harbour.

Thomas Ross (Tom) STENNING Wing. Born St Leonard's, Sydney 1892. Died Ryde, Sydney 1971 (aged 79). Corporal 31st Infantry Battalion. Lived most of his life in Willoughby, North Sydney. Plasterer. Married and enlisted in 1916.

Peter Neave BUCHANAN Five-eighth. Born Wellington (New Zealand) 11/1/1889. Died 30/1/1957. Glebe-Balmain/NSW (1919-23). 1 cap (1923). Company Sergeant-Major 19th and 3rd Battalions, 12th Reinforcements. Captain of the Trench team. Went from Palmerston North in New Zealand to enlist at Holsworthy, NSW. Captain Metropolitan v South Africa 1921. Goalkicker.

Jack Cosgrove (Bluey) WATKINS Five-eighth. Born 1893. Died 13/7/1974, aged 82. Private, 2nd Divisional Ammunition Column. Played Rugby League for Eastern Suburbs and Australia (7 caps), including tour to GB 1921-22.

Thomas W (Rat) FLANAGAN Scrum half. From Murwillumbah, NSW. Private in 9th Infantry Battalion. Aged 16 when he enlisted, but he lied about his age and was accepted. He also fought in WW2 despite being told he was too old! Played Rugby League for Brisbane Wests/Queensland (1919-21).

William Thornton (Bill) WATSON, MC, DCM, DSO Forward. Born Nelson (New Zealand) 10/11/1887. Died New York (USA) 9/9/1961. Newtown (46 games)/NSW (20 games)/Sydney (59 games)/Glebe-Balmain (13 games)/ Drummoyne. Moved to Sydney in 1911. 8 caps (1912-1920). Lieutenant. Military Cross (August 1918) and bar (October 1918) and DCM (at the Somme) in WW1. Gunner at Gallipoli and Western Front, but wounded in Belgium 1917. DSO in WW2 at Kokoda Track when Major of Papuan Infantry Battalion. He was later the Australian vice-consul in New York. Also a Plantation Manager. Toured USA in 1912 and New Zealand in 1913. He was covered in festering sores from Mustard Gas in WW1.

John Herbert BOND, MSM Hooker. Born Newcastle, NSW 1892. Wickham Public School/Glebe-Balmain/Drummoyne/Norths/Newcastle/NSW (16 games) Quarter-master/Sergeant in 30th Battalion. 4 caps (1920-21). Carpenter. Awarded the Meritorious Service Medal in July 1918. Toured New Zealand 1921.

Arthur M (Budget) LYONS Forward. Queensland and later a Queensland selector. Private 15th Infantry Battalion.

Ernest Austin S (Bill) CODY Forward. Born Melbourne 1889. Died 1968. St Joseph's College, Sydney/Eastern Suburbs/Randwick/NSW. 3 caps (1913). Lieutenant 5th Field Ambulance. He injured a leg in the Services game against Queensland later in 1919 and never played again. Toured New Zealand 1913.

William Roger BRADLEY Forward. NSW. Corporal, then Sgt. 13th Infantry Battalion.

John (Bluey) THOMPSON Forward. Born Warwick (Queensland) 15/7/1886. Died 1978. Brothers RFC, Brisbane/Toowoomba Brothers/ Queensland. Private, then Lance-Corporal in 15th Field Ambulance. 2 caps (1914). Farmer.

Joseph MURRAY, DCM Forward. Sergeant 7th Field Company Engineers. Played Rugby League for Newtown (pre-war), North Sydney (post-war) and for Australia on tour of GB 1911-12.

Godfrey Edward SEE, MM Forward. NSW (1919). Sergeant 33rd Infantry Battalion. Gained the Military Medal (13/8/1918).

Additionally, for the game v South Africa:

James Harry (Jimmy) BOSWARD Centre. Wentworth RFC (captain and coach)/NSW (1913-19). Gunner in 14th Battalion 5th Field Artillery.

Horace Randolph POUNTNEY Wing. Born Moree NSW 23/5/1891. Died Newcastle, NSW 1966. Shipping Clerk. Played for NSW. Lieutenant. 7th Field Artillery Brigade, 26th Battery. Married 1924. One brother survived war, but another KIA 1915.

Walter F (Wally) MATTHEWS Fly half. Born Orange, NSW 1884. Died 1954. Major. Formed and managed the side and had to play occasionally. NSW (1906-1910). Mayor of Orange 1936-44 and 1948-50. Managed Australia to SA in 1933. He was a doctor.

Thomas QUINN Forward. Private. Played Rugby League for Newcastle (NSW).

Vivian Alphonsus (Viv) DUNN Front-Row Forward. Born Junee, NSW 1895. Glebe-Balmain, then changed name to Drummoyne/ Southern Districts/NSW (15 games, 1919-21). Corporal in 1st Field Company Engineers. 7 caps (1920-21). Carpenter. Moved to Wide Bay, Queensland. Toured New Zealand 1921.

Additionally, for the game v the RAF:

Mick (Pat) EGAN Wing. Lance-Corporal, then Sergeant 26th Infantry Battalion.

Stanley (Stan) RYAN Fly half. Played for Brisbane Wests/Queensland. Lieutenant 3rd Motor Group Brigade. Circulation Manager of the Brisbane Telegraph. Became an Australian RU selector.

Additionally, for the game v Canada:

Daniel Brendan (Dan) CARROLL Centre, also wing and scrum half. Born Melbourne but various dates suggesting 1888 to 1892. Died San Francisco (USA) 5/8/1956. St Aloysius College, Sydney/Stanford University/USA/St George's, Sydney/NSW/ New Zealand Universities/ Neath (1 game). 2 caps for Australia (1908-12). He won Olympic rugby golds for Australia in 1908 and USA in 1920. Toured with Australia to USA in 1912 and Stanford University to New Zealand in 1913. Studied Dentistry/Oil Company Executive and USA football coach. Served in the USA Army and was a Lieutenant in the Australian Army, then emigrated to USA in 1920. In the 1908 Olympics he was said to be 16 years 169 days old.

John ROBERTSON Fly half. 14th Field Ambulance, then Gunner 104th Howitzer Battery.

Additionally, for the previously-postponed game v NZ:

James C (Jimmy) CLARKEN Hooker. Born Thames (New Zealand) 19/7/1876. Died Sydney 31/7/1953. Glebe (club record 140 apps.)/ Drummoyne/Randwick/NSW (24 games 1904-12). Army Driver, 4th Mechanical Transport Service. Australia tour to New Zealand in 1905 and USA in 1912. 4 caps (1905-1910). Goldminer, then Car Hire owner. Noted surf-lifesaver, he took part in a mass rescue at Maroubra Beach (Sydney) in 1910, rescuing ten people and bringing four bodies to shore. He played for NSW in three games against the GB tourists of 1904. In the King's Cup NZ persisted with a two-man front row. He stuck his head between them and secured the loose head for the AIF, no matter which side the ball was put in. He was nearly 43 at this time, and then toured with the AIF team in Australia!

Jimmy Clarken

4.2   CANADA

Beyond the details of who played for them, and in which of their five King's Cup matches, further information of any kind about the Canadian Services rugby personnel has to date proved very hard to come by. More would be much welcomed, including, one suspects, by those in British Columbia and beyond who are keen to fill out the sketchy history of early Canadian rugby.

The histories and websites have only one sentence on Canada's wartime rugby – *'little rugby was played during the years of World War I, when many men who had been active in the game joined the armed forces, but some did play overseas for regimental sides or for the Canadian Expeditionary Force team in 1919.'*

This paucity is the more regrettable since rugby in Canada has an intriguing early history. Its likely 1860s beginnings, with British sailors and Vancouver locals, were followed by the first organised sides, including university teams, and boosted when American football fell into disfavour

Toronto Varsity Rugby

5127. Upper Canada College, Toronto.

Early 1900s Toronto Rugby

with many US colleges and universities in 1905. Rugby became the game of choice at Stanford University, the University of California and several other 'Sunshine State' colleges. There were annual exchanges between Victoria, Vancouver and the two US universities until 1913, while varsity rugby also flourished at Toronto for a time.

British Columbia was also a favourite destination for the early

The All Blacks at Vancouver, 1913

'British Lions' Anglo-Welsh (1908), Australian (1909), New South Wales (1912) and New Zealand (1913) touring sides before World War One, though Vancouver's first two matches outside Canada, both predictably lost, were against New Zealand in 1906 in Berkeley and San Francisco.

Canadian football, their home-grown variety more akin to American football, had meanwhile developed quite widely in that huge land, alongside, or instead of, rugby.

Vancouver v Berkeley at Brockton Oval

The early Canadian Rugby Football Union, formed in 1884, was to become instead the administrators of that distinctive brand of oval ball sport.

In 1919, then, there seems to have been no effective national governing body with whom the Canadian Services could have liaised even had they wanted or needed to. (Many clubs in many countries may occasionally and temporarily have envied such a position!) It was to be a decade later that Rugby Union of Canada became established in 1929.

However the King's Cup was, in any case and of necessity, very much a Services competition, and those chosen to represent Canada at this 'top table' of rugby seem to have done so with verve and determination, whatever the odds. For all but a few of the 33 who seem to have turned out in their colours, the sum of what we have to record is their name and any comment on individual performances gleaned from the newspapers of the day.

Those 33 were:

In Canada's first game, v New Zealand:

Corporal F HOLLAND Full back

Sapper James H (Jimmy) Pritchard Wing. Winnipeg Welsh. 101st Battalion.

Lieutenant Edward Wallace Waits WATLING, MC & Bar Centre. Born 16/03/1888 Chatham, New Brunswick. 10th Brigade, 145th Battalion, Canadian Infantry. Wounded winning Bar to earlier MC at Arieux, 12/10/1918. Grocer and, in 1929, Mayor of Chatham. In 1985 he was posthumously inducted into the New Brunswick Sports Hall of Fame as the best all-round athlete ever produced along the Miramichi River (Nth New Brunswick). He was to die of meningitis in 1929, aged 41. Scored the Canadians' only try of the tournament. His son, Lloyd, also won the MC, in WW2.

Captain Almond Marcus GRIMMETT, MC Centre. Infantry Battalion. Born 6/10/1893 Boisrevain, Manitoba. Died 9/4/1983 Vancouver. Educated at Vancouver High School/Vancouver College (became University of British Columbia). Played rugby and basketball for College (Captain of rugby 1912-13). Enlisted in Vancouver in the 29th Battalion Canadian Expeditionary Force. After the war he rowed and played rugby for Vancouver Rowing Club.

Corporal J D PHILLIPS Wing

Lance-Corporal George EDWARDS (Captain) Fly half

Lieutenant Carl Campbell KENNING Scrum half. Born 25/5/1890 Victoria (BC). Died 8/6/1929 Vancouver (BC). Married Doris Harriett Evans in 1912. British Columbia. Canadian Artillery.

Private Matthew A HALL Forward. Private in Canadian Infantry. Emigrated to Canada 1907. Formerly with Westoe RFC/Durham County (Championship winners 1906-07)

Sergeant F A HERMAN Forward. Born 8/7/1889 Preston, Ontario. Died 6/1/1959. Served in the Mounted Rifles & 77th Battalion. Became Lieutenant and Captain. Bookkeeper.

Quartermaster-Sergeant Major J C SHINE Forward

Sergeant F DOBBS Forward

Lieutenant **R WILSON** Forward

Private **H E BRENNAN** Forward

Quartermaster-Sergeant Major **H YEOMAN** Forward

Major **H D DEEDES** Forward

Additionally, for the game v South Africa:

Lance-Corporal Arthur **VICKERY** Centre. Born 12/5/1894 Milverton, Somerset (GB). 73rd Battalion.

Private Septimus Basil **RICHARDSON** Wing. Born 17/11/1895 Malton, Yorkshire (GB). 151st Battalion.

Sergeant **H J McDONALD** Forward

Corporal **T McQUARRIE** Forward

Lieutenant John Charles **WAKEFIELD** Forward. Born Dundalk (Ireland) 13/4/1890. Served in the Infantry Battalion/2nd Canadian Division Cavalry. Boilermaker. His mother lived in Eastbourne (GB).

Lieutenant **H P McGUINGAN** Forward

Additionally, for the game v the Mother Country:

Private **EVANS** Full back

Corporal **C H PERRY** Wing

Private **E J HELLINGS** Scrum half

Sergeant Major **GUTHRIE** Forward

Additionally, for the game v Australia:

Sergeant-Major Samuel J (Sammy) DAVIES Fly half. Winnipeg. Brother of Dai.

Sergeant-Major David (Dai) DAVIES Scrum half. Winnipeg. Brother of Sammy.

Lieutenant COCHRANE Forward

Private WHITE Forward

Sergeant-Major A M NISBET Forward

Additionally, for the game v the RAF:

Sergeant LIGHT Forward

Sergeant HOUSON (or Henson) Forward

Sergeant Franklyn Arthur HERMAN (or Norman) Forward

4.3   FRANCE

France was involved in the King's Cup only to the extent that the winners of the tournament were then to play against their recent Allies from across the English Channel in a challenge match at Twickenham.

Until this time French rugby, introduced there by British residents in the 1870s, had been run as part of the *Union des Sociétés Françaises de Sports Athlétiques*, and it was not until just after World War One that the FFR, the *Fédération Français de Rugby*, was formed.

While the south-west was to become French rugby's stronghold and the heartland of its heady blend of ferocity and flair, it was two rival Paris teams, *Racing Club de France* (1882) and *Stade Français* (1883) who contested the first ever French rugby union championship on March 20, 1892. The game was refereed by Olympic founder Baron Pierre de Coubertin and saw Racing win 4–3.

In 1900, rugby was played at the Paris Olympics. France, along with Germany and Great Britain, entered and the hosts won the first ever Olympic rugby gold medals. In 1905, England and France played each other for the first time, and the *'Tricolores'* soon began to play the four home countries on an almost regular (though rarely, at that stage, victorious) basis up to 1914.

It was apparently the French who coined the phrase 'five nations' for the championship from 1910 on, but in their first four years of entry, the French won just one match – a one point victory over Scotland at Stade Colombes in 1911.

Rugby was again played at the 1920 Olympics, though this time, in one of the most surprising results in rugby history, France failed in the gold medal match, being defeated 8-0 by the United States. France again participated in rugby at the 1924 Olympics – the last time 15-a-side rugby was played as an Olympic sport – when the USA successfully defended their title.

The side for the game at Twickenham on April 19th, 1919 included the following eight players who were, or became French internationals:

Jean ETCHEBERRY Wing, later Back Row. Born Boucau 27/8/1901. Died Les Cotes d'Arey 5/2/1982. Rochefort/Cognac/Vienne. 16 caps (1923-27). Played in the 1924 Olympics. Sergeant-Major.

Rene CRABOS Centre. Born St Sever, Cote Basque 7/2/1899. Died St Sever 17/6/1964. Joinville Military School (Paris)/Mont de Marsan/Dax/Tarbes/Racing Club de France/St Sever. 17 caps (1920-24). Played in the 1920 Olympics and was manager of several French tours. Broke leg against Ireland in Dublin, 1924. Manager of French tours to Argentina 1949, 1954 and 1960. FFR President (1952-62).

Rene Crabos

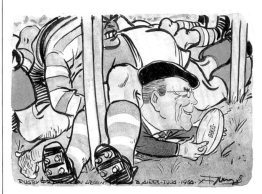

Crabos as President of the FFR

Philippe STRUXIANO Fly half. Born Toulouse 11/3/1891. Died Toulouse 21/4/1956. Toulouse/Avignon (player-coach). 7 caps (1913-20). Captain of the side. Agricultural chemical producer.

Skipper Philippe Struxiano

Robert THIERRY Forward. Born Brienon-sur-Armancon 23/6/1893. Died Valence-en-Brie 21/10/1973. 4 caps (1920). Sub-Lieutenant who lost an eye in WW1. Played in the 1920 Olympics. Teacher at a vets school. Committee, then President of Toulouse.

Fernand VAQUER Forward. Born La Tourbas-Elne 22/6/1889. Died Tresserre 17/9/1979. Perpignan/Toulouse/Racing Club. Coach of Perpignan. 3 caps (1921-22). Sergeant-Major in the French Army 23rd Artillery Regiment.

Pierre PONS Forward. Born Llupia 16/9/1894. Died Toulouse 24/2/1981. Played for AS Perpignan/Toulouse. 6 caps (1920-22). Sergeant in the French Army.

Eugène SOULIÉ Forward. Born Paris July 1898. Died 21/6/1927. CASG club. Played in the 1920 Olympics. 8 caps (1920-22). Died aged just 28.

It is assumed that Private CASSOUJET in the forwards was in fact:

Aime CASSAYET. Died Narbonne 26/5/1927 (though, like so many players, especially forwards, he appears to have had a 'programme age'. His birth and age differ from 28 to 34!). 31 caps (1920-27). He played in the 1924 Olympics and captained France in eight matches, sadly all lost. He died just three months after his last cap, having contracted a serious illness. He played for Tarbes and Narbonne and had been taken prisoner of war in 1914. His name has also been shown as Cassayet-Armagnac.

'Wakers' with Aime Cassayet in the 20's

The seven who did not obtain international honours were:

Sergeant MAZARICO Full back

Lieutenant RIEU Centre

Major/Adjutant (Doctor) LOUBATIE Wing

Sub-Lieutenant DUSSERT Scrum half

Major DILLESEGER Forward

Sub-Lieutenant GALLIAX Forward

Sub-Lieutenant NICOLAI Forward

Again not unusually, the press spelling of several other players' names appears to be inconsistent, with Rieu also shown as Recu and Mazarico as Mazarice.

BOYAU (×), CAPITAINE DE L'ÉQUIPE DE FRANCE DE RUGBY CONTRE L'ARMÉE ZÉLANDAISE EN 1917

A French XV who played a NZ XV in 1917. Maurice Boyau, French captain, was a flying ace who lost his life in September 1918

4.4   MOTHER COUNTRY

Rather than try to select national sides from the four home countries from amongst the military ranks, the single British Army opted to select a single British side to represent the 'Mother Country'.

It was highly unusual to see a rugby team chosen to represent the whole of the British Isles other than in an overseas touring context. True, the Barbarians, a marvellous law unto themselves from Day One, selected players from all parts: but to represent not Britain, but the Club. They did not play against an overseas country, either, until Australia, almost by accident, in 1948.

The tours from Britain to Australia, New Zealand and South Africa now labelled as the pioneering ventures of the British 'Lions' were not yet given that nickname, nor were they generally selected from the breadth nor, often, the very best of Britain (which, of course, just about included Ireland, at that stage).

The earliest treks to the southern hemisphere date back to 1888, the first having been a commercial venture undertaken without official backing, when a 21-man squad from England, Scotland and Wales visited Australia and New Zealand. The six subsequent visits enjoyed a growing degree of support from the authorities, before the 1910 South Africa tour became the first official tour representative of the four Home Unions.

In 1891, and sanctioned by the Rugby Football Union, the English national team, though others referred to it as the British Isles, toured South Africa. Five years later a British Isles side revisited, with a squad having a notable Irish orientation, the Irish national team contributing six players to the 21-man party. Then in 1899 a British Isles touring side returned to Australia, the squad of 23 having, for the first time ever, players from each of the home nations.

In 1903, there was another visit to South Africa. The British side lost the test series, drawing twice, but with the hosts winning the decider 8-0. The 1904 venture to Australia and New Zealand saw the tourists devastate the Australian teams, but manage only two early New Zealand wins before losing the test and winning just once more, with a further draw.

On the 1908 tour there were more matches in New Zealand than in Australia. The Anglo-Welsh side (the Irish and Scottish unions did not participate) performed well in the non-test matches, and drew one NZ test but lost the other two.

The 1910 South Africa tour, selected by a committee from the four Home Unions, marked the beginning, then, of British and Irish rugby tours 'proper'. The team performed moderately in the non-test games, claiming victories in just over half: the test series, however, went to South Africa, who won two of the three games.

Between 1905 and 1913, meanwhile, all three major southern hemisphere sides had toured the UK, South Africa twice. Their strength, with Australia a little behind the other two, was not in doubt. So, while the teams in 1919 were restricted to those who had taken up arms, the relaxation on rugby league players' eligibility could boost their already-impressive ranks and the Mother Country could expect a mighty challenge.

The players chosen to meet it were:

In their first game, v Australia:

Barry Stephenson CUMBERLEGE, OBE Full back. Born Jesmond, Newcastle-on-Tyne 5/6/1891. Died Sandgate, Folkestone 22/9/1970. Durham School/Cambridge University/Blackheath/Sussex/ Northumberland/Barbarians. England 8 caps (1920-22). OBE 1918. Twice mentioned in despatches. Refereed 16 internationals (1926-34). Major in RASC, later New Zealand Division. Lloyd's underwriter. Was an Observer, Army Service Corps of the 3rd Cavalry Division in WW2.

Cambridge Blues at rugby 1910-13 and cricket 1913, also played cricket for Durham, Northumberland and Kent (1923-24).

Harold Lindsay Vernon DAY. Born Darjeeling, Bengal, India 12/8/1898. Died Hadley Wood, Hertfordshire 15/6/1972. Bedford Modern School/ Leicester/Army/ Midlands/Royal Artillery/ Leicestershire/Hampshire. England 4 caps (1920-26), scored 2 tries, 2 cons, 1 pen.

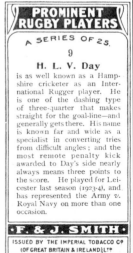

F. & J. SMITH'S CIGARETTES.

PROMINENT RUGBY PLAYERS

A SERIES OF 25.

9

H. L. V. Day

is as well known as a Hampshire cricketer as an International Rugger player. He is one of the dashing type of three-quarter that makes straight for the goal-line—and generally gets there. His name is known far and wide as a specialist in converting tries from difficult angles; and the most remote penalty kick awarded to Day's side nearly always means three points to the score. He played for Leicester last season (1923-4), and has represented the Army v. Royal Navy on more than one occasion.

H. L. V. DAY
LEICESTER & ENGLAND.

F. & J. SMITH

ISSUED BY THE IMPERIAL TOBACCO C° (OF GREAT BRITAIN & IRELAND) L^{TD}

Harold Day Cigarette Card, 1920s

Refereed one Victory international. Schoolmaster. Lieutenant in the Royal Artillery. Hampshire cricket (80 matches). Scored 1,151 points for Leicester 1919-29 with 108 tries, 281 cons, 81 pens, 4 drop goals, 2 goals from a mark.

William John CULLEN, MBE Centre. Born Balghupar, India 7/12/1894. Died St Ives, Huntingdonshire 28/6/1960. Christ's Hospital School/Oxford University (no Blue)/Monkstown/Manchester/Barbarians. Ireland 1 cap (1920). Second Lieut/ Lieutenant/Captain in 7th Battalion, Leicestershire Regiment. Played cricket in India.

Reginald Clarence Werrett (Reg) PICKLES, MC Centre, and also full back. Born Keynsham, Bristol 11/12/1895. Died 6/11/1978. Weston-super-Mare. Lieutenant. Bristol Grammar School/Bristol/Clifton/Gloucestershire. Military Cross in 1917. England 2 caps at full back in 1922. Captained Bristol in 1920-21 and 1921-22, playing 244 games for the club. Served in Royal Engineers.

Reg Pickles

Charles William Rivers PANTLIN Wing. Born 15/12/1887 Stepney. Died 1978 Hastings. Lieutenant, then Captain in the Army (Royal Field Artillery). Lived in Exeter and Swiss Cottage, London. United Services/Ireland Trials (pre-war) but uncapped/Richmond/ London Irish. Member of Lloyd's and a director of a roofing company.

John Morris Clement (Clem) LEWIS Fly half. Born: Bridgend 22/6/1890. Died: Porthcawl 25/10/1944. Wales 11 caps (1912-23). For Wales (pre and post-war) he scored three tries, three conversions and a drop goal (19 points) and was captain in his last two appearances in 1923 (both were losses). He also played for Wales against the Barbarians in 1915 when he dropped a goal. He attended Bridgend County School and played for Porthcawl and Bridgend (1907-08 and 1908-09) before going up to St Catharine's College, Cambridge and winning Blues in 1913 and 1919. He appeared for Handsworth RFC, London Welsh and Crawshay's and then for Cardiff 229 times from 1909-10 until 1923-24. He scored 62 tries and 11 drop goals and was captain in 1920-21. In

WW1 he was a Lieutenant in the Cardiff City Battalion of the Welch Regiment, being gassed and wounded. He was a colliery salesman, then a schoolmaster in Cornelly and was in the Civil Defence in WW2 before dying suddenly at his Porthcawl home.

John Alfred PYM, MC Scrum half. Born Kingston 25/3/1891. Died Auckland (NZ) 9/2/1969. Cheltenham College (1907-09)/RMA Woolwich/Army/Blackheath/ Kent/Barbarians. England 4 caps (1912). Captain in the Royal Artillery, wounded, mentioned in despatches twice. Military Cross & Bar. Emigrated to New Zealand as a farmer. The Times reported him as dead in 1917, but later apologised. He lived for another 52 years!

Charles Milne USHER, DSO, OBE Forward. Born Wimbledon 26/9/1891. Died Haddington 21/1/1981. Merchiston Castle School/RMA Sandhurst/US Portsmouth/Army/London Scottish/Edinburgh Wanderers/Barbarians. Scotland 16 caps (1912-22). Captain in the Gordon Highlanders. He was a PoW for four and a half years after the Battle of Mons. Played for Scotland while on honeymoon and in 1922 he piped Scotland onto the field. He also fenced for Scotland. Director of Physical Education at Edinburgh University (1946-59). Colonel in the Gordon Highlanders in WW2. Croix de Guerre avec Palms and DSO at Dunkirk. He took charge of the Scotland team in the 1950, 1954 and 1958 Empire Games.

Joseph BRUNTON, MC, DSO Forward. Born Tynemouth 21/8/1888. Died Hammersmith 18/9/1971. Newcastle Grammar School/North Durham/Rockcliff/ Northumberland/Army. Chairman & Managing Director of an Energy Company. Served in the Seaforth Highlanders, then Lieutenant-Colonel in the Northumberland Fusiliers. Military Cross in 1916 and Bar in 1917. Mentioned in despatches three times. England 3 caps (1914). President RFU 1953-54. Refereed an international in 1925.

Charles Henry (Cherry) PILLMAN, MC Forward. Born Sidcup January 1890. Died Bromley-by-Bow 13/11/1955. Tonbridge School/Blackheath/Kent/Barbarians/ GB. England 18 caps (1910-14). GB to SA 1910 (2 tests). Lieutenant then Captain in Dragoon Guards. Flour importer/London Corn Exchange. Was an Area Flour officer in WW2. Remarkably fast, athletic, back row scoring star of 1910 tour.

Alexander Richard V SYKES, MC, DSO Forward. Born Birkenhead 29/5/1891. Died Hampshire c.1977. Birkenhead Sch/Liverpool University/Blackheath (38 games 1912-14)/Barbarians. England 1 cap (1914). Major in King's Liverpool Regiment (Army).

Leonard (or Lionel) Graham (Leo, Bruno) BROWN, MC Forward. Born Brisbane 6/9/1888. Died Charing Cross Hosp 23/5/1950. Brisbane Grammar School/Oxford University/London Hosp/Surrey/Blackheath/Barbarians. England 18 caps (1911-22), once as capt. Captain, Lt-Colonel, then Colonel, RAMC. MC in 1917. Mentioned in despatches 1918. Doctor/consulting surgeon/ENT specialist.

'Bruno' Brown

Rev William Thomas (Bill) HAVARD, MC Forward. Born Defynnog, Breconshire 23/10/1889. Died Gwbert, Ceredigion 17/8/1956. Brecon County Secondary School/University College, Aberystwyth/Oxford University/Llanelli/London Welsh. Wales 1 cap (1919 v New Zealand Army). From Aberystwyth University he went to St Michael's Theological College, Llandaff in Cardiff to become an Army chaplain in the War where he was mentioned in despatches and gained the DSO in 1916 and was awarded the Military Cross in 1918 for bravery. He went to Jesus College, Oxford, gaining a 1919 Blue alongside his college, university and Wales pack teammate Gwyn Francis. He played soccer for Aberystwyth and Swansea Town, scoring the latter's first goal in competitive football in 1912 and also notched Llanelli's first try (against the New Zealand Army) after war had ended. He became Curate of Brecon, Vicar of Hook, St Luke's (Battersea) and St Mary's (Swansea), then Canon of Brecon Cathedral, Bishop of St Asaph and finally St David's. His preaching took him as far as Yale University (USA). Died at 66 and was buried at Brecon. In late 1919, while playing in a Jesus College trial match, as Havard passed he was tackled by Geoffrey Goddard, but Havard fell on him and Goddard died. The inquest found it was an accident.

William George K FINDLAY Hooker/Forward. Born Clackmannanshire c.1895. Captain in the Royal Field Artillery. Glasgow Academicals. 3rd Lowland (Field Ambulance) Brigade, Royal Field Artillery, then 1st Battalion King's Own Scottish Borderers. One of only two members of this team against Australia not to be capped, it appears.

Robert Arthur **GALLIE, MC** Forward. Born Edinburgh 18/1/1893. Died Edinburgh 25/5/1948. Glasgow Academy/Fettes College/Glasgow Academicals. Scotland 8 caps (1920-21). Flour Miller. Croix de Guerre in 1918. Military Cross in 1918. He was the father of three sons, of whom Major George Holmes Gallie, MC (1 cap 1939) and Lieutenant Robert Eric Gallie both died in WW2.

Additionally, for the game v the RAF:

Allen Thomson SLOAN, DSO Wing, later fly half. Born 30/12/1892. Died 2/10/1952. Edinburgh Academy/ Edinburgh Academicals/Edinburgh University/ Barbarians. Major in the Army. Doctor. Scotland 9 caps (1914-21). Father of Donald Allen Sloan (7 caps 1950-53).

Robert Sholto (Rob) HEDDERWICK, MC Born 6/7/1886 Kensington, London. Died 22/1/1941 Uckfield, Sussex. Forward. Major in the Army (Tank Corps). Lorretto School/London Scottish. Also schooled in Ware, Hertfordshire.

Charles William JONES Forward. Born 18/6/1893. Died Birkenhead 19/1/1960. Bridgend/Newport/Army/Harlequins/Leicester/ BirkenheadPark/Cardiff (1 game, 1913-14)/St Peter's (Cardiff). Company Sergeant Major in the Second Battalion, Welch Regiment. Physical Training instructor at Birkenhead School. Wales 3 caps (1920). Better known as CSM (Company Sergeant Major) Jones, he played for the Welch Regiment in five Army Cup finals. He was on the Army gymnastics staff and was the first non-officer in an Army representative or Mother Country team.

Additionally, for the game v Canada:

Arthur Douglas (Podger) LAING Forward. Born c.1892 Kincardineshire. Died 24/11/1927 (aged 55). Royal High School/Royal HSFP. Scotland 7 caps (1914-21). Second Lieutenant, later Captain in the Army – South Staffordshire Regiment and Royal Scots. He was a brewer.

Philip Henry (Peter) LAWLESS, MC Forward. Born 9/10/1891 Wandsworth. Died 10/3/1945, killed by German shell nr Remagen Bridge in WW2. Bedford Grammar Sch/Richmond/Middlesex/Surrey/Devon/

Army/Barbarians/England Trial (1921). Daily Telegraph writer who was correspondent with the RAF, then joined the Army Intelligence Corps, but returned to the Telegraph as a war correspondent, mainly with the American First Army. He represented London Rowing Club at eights. Military Cross in WW1 as a Major in the 18th Middlesex Regiment. Wrote the posthumously-published *'Rugger's An Attacking Game' (Sampson Low, 1946)*. It has been suggested that Peter Lawless' experiences during World War One, were drawn upon by his grandson, Sebastian Faulks, during the writing of his award-winning bestselling novel *Birdsong (Hutchinson, 1993)*.

No new players were introduced for the NZ match, but additionally, for the game v South Africa:

James Alfred Nicholson DICKSON Wing. Born Enniskillen 12/3/1897. Died Fermanagh County Hospital 24/11/1963. Portora Royal School/ Trinity College, Dublin. Ireland 3 caps (1920). Dental Surgeon. Lieutenant in the Army – Loyal Inniskilling Fusiliers (3rd Battalion).

Herbert B MOORE Forward. Born Downpatrick 8/6/1890. Died Hastings 1976. Royal School Dungannon/Queen's University, Belfast/ Uppingham School/Oxford University (Brasenose College). Ireland 8

Programme Cover, Mother Country v Canada

caps (1910-12, debut aged 19 yrs 263 days). Major in the King's Own Scottish Borderers. He was Oxford University's captain in 1919, but withdrew to take a job.

No new players were introduced for the play-off game v New Zealand.

This cigarette card looks very much as if it could be the Mother Country v NZ at Twickenham 1919, but is in fact from Stephen Mitchell & Son, 1907, and seems to be Dave Gallaher tackling Gwyn Nicholls, opposing All Blacks and Welsh skippers in the epic 1905 clash at Cardiff, four years before 'Twickers' was opened.

4.5   NEW ZEALAND

The impact of the magnificent 'Originals', the 1905 'All Blacks' who had taken these islands by storm, and their subsequent performances at home against tourists, meant that although South Africa, later, were often to prove superior on their own soil, New Zealand were already seen as the nation against which to judge the rugby of the rest.

Their response, along with the other Dominions, to the call of the Empire in the war had only enhanced their reputation, although on the rugby front some amongst other Unions' committees and the press found their will to win, 'adaptations' of the rules and alleged flirtations with the professional game hard to swallow.

The New Zealand contribution is perhaps best embodied in the life and death of the Irish-born captain of those almost-invincible pioneers of 1905, Dave Gallaher. (Their only defeat, of course, in 35 matches, was that immortal 3-0 Welsh win at Cardiff: mercifully, Bob Deans' disallowed equalizing 'try' could not then be referred to a TMO - a television match official!)

Great forward, leader, writer and thinker on the game, Gallaher had 'reduced' his age in signing up in 1901 for action with the New Zealand Contingent in the Anglo-Boer War: and again in 1916 when, officially exempt, he enlisted with the New Zealand Division for service in WW1. He was killed at Passchendaele the following year.

Like Wales at the same period, New Zealand found rugby prowess a badge of pride and a source of international recognition for a small nation. The enduring expectation of excellence became both a focus for national endeavour on the field, and an additional burden for those seeking to maintain and burnishing it.

As the Taranaki newspaper quoted earlier made very evident, it was anticipated and demanded that the New Zealand Services side in the King's Cup should deliver a performance worthy of its nation's rugby traditions: and, of course, win.

Those who strove to do so were:

Dave Gallaher

In their first game, v the RAF:

Charles H (Charlie) CAPPER, MM Full back. Private, Corporal, then Bombardier in Field Artillery. Played for Samoa against Fiji in 1924. He survived the sinking of the Maquette on October 23, 1915 when many died. Was a back row forward at Wellington College, NZ. Awarded the Military Medal in April 1918.

William August (Jockey) FORD Wing. Born Christchurch 25/8/1895. Died Christchurch 7/7/1959. Papanui Primary School/West Christchurch/Canterbury/ Merivale RFC/South Island. Private, later Sergeant in the Rifle Brigade. A drover. Including games against NSW, he played nine times for New Zealand: no 'Tests'.

Charlie Capper at College, 1909

'Jockey' Ford

Career on a card

Leonard B (Jack) STOHR Centre. Born New Plymouth 13/11/1889. Died Springs, near Johannesburg (South Africa) 25/7/1973. West End School/Central School/New Plymouth Boys High School/Tukapa/Taranaki/ North Island. Chemist. Moved to South Africa in 1920. 3 caps (1910). Private, later Sergeant in the Medical Corps.

Percival Wright (Percy) STOREY Wing. Born Temuka 11/2/1897. Died Timaru 4/10/1975. Waimate School/Timaru Zingari/South Canterbury/ South Island. Two caps (1921). Toured NSW 1920. Sergeant, then Staff-Sergeant in the Otago Infantry Regiment. Wounded at Passchendaele. Traveller. Sports Officer at Burnham Camp in WW2.

Gifford John (Jack) McNAUGHT, DSO Five-eighth. Born Wanganui 26/11/1896. Died New Plymouth 1/6/1975. Played for Otago. Student who became Sergeant, then 2nd Lieutenant in the Machine Gun Corps in WW1 and Lieutenant-Colonel in the 25th Battalion in WW2, then Captain/Major in Wellington Regiment. Victoria University College (Wellington), then Otago University and representative on the New Zealand University RU Committee in 1924. Became headmaster of New Plymouth Boys High School (1942-57). DSO at Sidi Rezegh 23/11/1941 when wounded.

William Reginald (Bill) FEA Five-eighth. Born Dunedin 5/10/1898. Died Trevellyn Hospital, Hamilton 22/12/1988. Otago Boys High School/ University RFC/New Zealand Universities/Otago/ South Island. 1 cap (1921). Private, later Sergeant in the Rifle Brigade. Lieutenant-Colonel in 8th and 24th Field Ambulance in WW2. New Zealand squash champion 1936-37. Doctor. Lived in England in the 1930s. Invited to captain New Zealand in 1923 but declined due to his medical studies.

Charles (Chas) BROWN Scrum half. Born New Plymouth 19/12/1887. Died New Plymouth 2/4/1966. Central School/New Plymouth Star RFC/ Tukapa RFC/ Taranaki/North Island. 2 caps (1913). First non-Maori to play for the NZ Maori team. Corporal, then Staff-Sergeant in Field Engineers. New Zealand selector 1947-48. After player poll, elected captain of the New Zealand Army team to South Africa in 1919.

Charles Brown

Arthur Percy (Singy) SINGE Forward. Auckland. Private, later Sergeant in the Auckland Infantry Regiment. Turned to rugby league in New Zealand after the War and won two caps at that code in 1925-26. After he died it was found that he had shrapnel in his head.

Edward William (Nut) HASELL Forward. Born Christchurch 26/4/1889. Died Christchurch 7/4/1966. National School in Christchurch/ Merivale RFC/Matakanui RFC/Otago/South Island. 2 caps (1913). Bombardier, later Staff-Sergeant in New Zealand Field Artillery. Law/ brewery secretary/accountant.

R SELLARS Forward. Sapper in Divisional Signals, later Sergeant. Stevenage Camp.

Leslie J COCKCROFT Forward. Southland/Otago/South Canterbury. Sergeant, later Staff Sergeant in the Field Artillery. His brother (Eric) played for New Zealand in 1913-14 and uncle (Sam) was an All Black in 1893-94.

'Moke' Belliss

Nathaniel Arthur (Ranji) WILSON Forward. Born Christchurch 18/5/1886. Died Lower Hutt 11/8/1953. Athletic RFC/ Wellington/North Island. 10 caps (1908-14). Not allowed on the tour to South Africa, classed as 'coloured' owing to his English/West Indian parentage. New Zealand selector 1924-25. Sergeant in Army (Rifle Brigade). Played for NZ Convalescent Hospital (Hornchurch) in 1918. See also Chapter 7.

Jack KISSICK Forward. Taranaki. Sapper, later Sergeant in the Field Engineers.

Ernest Arthur (Moke) BELLISS Loose forward. Born Bunnythorpe, Palmerston North 1/4/1894. Died Taihape 22/4/1974. Wanganui/Moawhanga Huia RFC/ Hautapu RFC/North Island. 3 caps (1921). Private, later Sergeant in the Otago Infantry Regiment. Butcher/farmer. Toured Australia as Captain in 1922.

Richard (Dick) FOGARTY, MM Forward. Born Matakanui 12/12/1891. Died at the Little Sisters of the Poor home in Brackville, Dunedin 9/9/1980, aged 88. Union RFC/Otago/Taranaki/Hawera RFC/Auckland/ College Rifles RFC. Sergeant, later Staff-Sergeant in the New Zealand Rifle Brigade. 2 caps (1921) – one as a wing forward and one as a hooker. Awarded Military Medal. Timber Firm worker/ Carpenter. Oldest All Black at the time of his death. He never married.

Additionally, for the game v Canada, when a mostly reserve XV was fielded:

William L (Bill) HENRY Wing. Canterbury. Private/later Sergeant. Bulford Regiment and Canterbury Infantry Regiment.

Edmond (Eddie) RYAN Centre. Born Petone 17/2/1891. Died Wainuiomata 29/8/1965. Petone RFC/ Wellington/ Fielding TCOB/ Manawatu/North Island. Bombardier, later Sergeant, in the Field Artillery. Brother Jim won 4 caps and skippered the side in the final. Boilermaker. One All Blacks game v NSW in 1921.

G L OWLES Wing. Corporal/Bombardier in the Field Artillery. Canterbury.

E Richard William (Dick) ROBERTS Wing/Centre. Born Manaia (Waimate Plains) 23/1/1889. Died Okaiawa 8/3/1973. Kaponga RFC/ Taranaki/Okaiawa RFC/ Hawera/North Island. Rifleman, then Sergeant in the Rifle Brigade. 5 caps (1913-14). Toured North America 1913 and Australia (as captain) in 1914. Farmer/racehorse owner.

E WATSON Five-eighth. Sergeant in the Wellington Infantry Regiment.

Donald McKay SANDMAN, MM Scrum half. Born Christchurch 3/11/1889. Died Christchurch 29/1/1973. Canterbury Rugby. Private, later Sergeant in the Canterbury Infantry Regiment. Cricket pre and post-war for New Zealand and Canterbury. Awarded the Military Medal in 1918.

Michael Joseph (Mick) CAIN Forward. Born Waitara 7/7/1885. Died New Plymouth 27/8/51. Taranaki/Clifton RFC/North Island. Private, later

Sergeant in the Otago Infantry Regiment. New Zealand tour to USA in 1913 and Australia in 1914. 4 caps (1913-14). Freezing works employee.

Samuel J STANDEN Forward. Wellington. Corporal/Gunner/later Sergeant in the Field Artillery.

Eric J NAYLOR Forward. Sergeant, later Staff Sergeant in the Otago Infantry Regiment. Mentioned in despatches. Scorer of the try in the 4-3 loss to Pill Harriers.

Alexander (Alex) GILCHRIST Forward. Wellington. Gunner, later Sergeant in the Field Artillery.

F P ARNOLD Forward. Born Otahuhu. Sergeant in the Auckland Infantry Regiment. Wounded 1916.

C W TEPENE, MM Forward. Sergeant in the Otago Infantry Regiment. Wounded 1918. Military Medal 1918.

A A (Snowy) LUCAS Forward. Auckland. Gunner, later Sergeant in the Field Artillery.

Additionally, for the game v South Africa:

John Gerald (Jack) O'BRIEN Full back. Born Wellington 9/12/1889. Died Kiwitahi 9/1/1958. Auckland Marist/Auckland/North Island. 1 cap (1914). Post and Telegraph employee and Farmer. Corporal, then Sergeant-Major in the Army (Divisional Signals). Broke his leg on tour to Australia 1913. HRH the Prince of Wales, said of O'Brien: "If I dropped my kitbag from the dome of St Paul's, O'Brien would catch it."

James (Jimmy) RYAN Five-eighth, also Full back. Born Masterton 8/2/1887. Died Fielding 17/7/1957. Fielding Technical College Old Boys/ Petone RFC/Wellington/ Manawatu/North Island. 4 caps (1910-14). Regimental Sergeant-Major, later Captain in Otago Infantry Regiment. Toured Australia 1910 and 1914. He was the brother of All Black Ed Ryan. Captained the side in several of the remaining games, but Charles Brown was chosen to skipper the team to tour South Africa.

No new players were introduced for the match with the Mother Country, but additionally, for the previously postponed game v Australia:

Hugh George (Torp) WHITTINGTON Forward. Born Hawera c.1886. Died Inglewood, Hawera 24/5/1959. Hawera/Taranaki (pre-war). Corporal, later Staff-Sergeant in the Second Battalion, New Zealand Rifle Brigade. He was wounded in 1917 and admitted to hospital, but returned to action. After the war he joined the New Zealand Referees Association. He was a bricklayer and borough councillor, who built the New Zealand War Memorial at Ohawe. His parents were born in England – his father in Coates, West Sussex and his mother in Solihull, Warwickshire. His brother, Lance-Corporal Horace Whittington, was killed at Gallipoli in 1915.

Additionally, for the play-off game v the Mother Country:

James Edward (Jim) MOFFITT Forward. Born Waikato 3/6/1889. Died Auckland 16/3/1964. St James RFC/Oriental RFC/Wellington/North Island. 3 caps (1921). Second Lieutenant, later Lieutenant in Auckland Infantry Regiment. Tailor's cutter, then hotel manager.

Alfred Herbert (Alf) WEST Forward. Born Inglewood 6/5/1893. Died Hawera 7/1/1934. Matapu School/Taranaki/Hawera RFC/North Island. 2 caps (1921). Gunner, later Sergeant in the Field Artillery. Gassed in War. He toured with New Zealand to Australia in 1920 and GB/ France/Canada in 1924-25. Fencing contractor.

Alf West

(Note that all these players were given higher ranks after the war and before the tour to South Africa).

4.6 ROYAL AIR FORCE

The RAF had only been founded in 1918, towards the end of World War One, by merging the Royal Flying Corps and the Royal Naval Air Service. The world's oldest air force independent of army or navy control, the newly-created RAF was also the most powerful air force in the world at its official 'birth', with over 20,000 aircraft and, including the Women's Royal Air Force, over 300,000 personnel.

As previously mentioned, in 1919 the RAF Rugby Union was in its absolute infancy. There was, though, no reason to believe that the products of the schools, universities and clubs who had joined the Army or Navy but subsequently become part of the new force would be any less able or motivated than their Army rivals.

Wavell Wakefield recalls: '... *During the summer of 1918 I left Cranwell and was transferred to the fleet, being posted to HMS Vindictive. After the Armistice was signed, I received a message from the Air Ministry in February 1919, ordering me to report to join the Air Force side which was being formed for the Inter-Services League.'*

Meanwhile, in the immediate aftermath of war the 'Senior Service', with its essentially seaborne duties, could not be expected to raise a properly representative team.

The RAF, then, got off the ground and did its level best to raise a competitive outfit for the challenge. Its players, with quite a cosmopolitan character, were:

In their first game, v New Zealand:

William (Billy) SEDDON Full back. Wigan rugby league (1911-21, 70 games, 71 points). Lieutenant, who had previously served in the Navy.

Captain James Ira Thomas (Taffy) JONES Wing. Captain 'Taffy' Jones, famous leading fighter ace of No 74 'Tiger' Squadron, persuaded virtually 'out of the crowd' on the day to play against New Zealand! Born Llanddowror 18 April, 1896. Died in hospital August 29th 1960, after a fall from a ladder at his Aberaeron home. Won the MM, the DSO, the DFC, the MC, and later still a bar to his DFC. He even received a

Russian medal, the Order of St George – one of his proudest moments, although he had very little idea how he had come by it. Later played for the RAF in their first win over the Army, and fly half for several first class clubs including London Welsh. Became a Wing Commander, and though his attempts to fly officially for the RAF in WW2 failed, frightened off a German Junkers 88 bomber during a raid on S Wales in 1940 when 'over age' and with his only weapon a Verey flare pistol! Wrote three books including *An Air Fighter's Scrapbook*, and *Tiger Squadron: The Story of 74 Squadron R.A.F. in Two World Wars*.

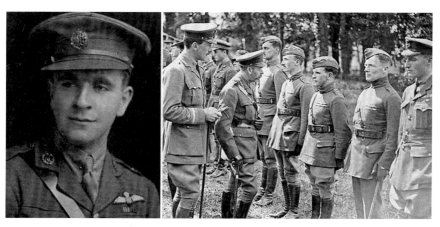

Capt Jones, above and (right), with King George V in France

Capt Jones, his wife and plane at St Clears, near his Welsh birthplace

WW Wakefield re-introduces the King to Jones (nearest camera), before the RAF's first win over the Army

Godfrey Maynard (Bai, George) WRENTMORE Centre/wing. Born Okiep, Namaqaland. 20/2/1893. Died Kenilworth, Cape Town 16/8/1953. Western Province. Nine games, no tests, on South African tour to GB in 1912. Lieutenant. Five first-class cricket matches for W Province, 1910/11 Currie Cup.

E N (or C D) FULLER Centre. It appears likely that it was Edward Newman Fuller (not Charles D Fuller) who played. Edward was born Billericay, Essex 25/9/1888 and died Hailsham, Sussex in September 1969. He was a Second Lieutenant, then Major in the Royal Flying Corps serving in France and Egypt. He played for Old Merchant Taylor's School (1906-07)/Magdalen College, Cambridge/OMT's (captain in 1910-11 and 1911-12)/Kent. GB tour to Argentina 1910. He played cricket at school (1903-07).

L H Tennant SLOAN Wing, later centre. Later Sir Tennant Sloan. Born 9/11/1884 Glasgow. Died Edinburgh 15/10/1972, Edinburgh

Academy/Edinburgh Academicals/Glasgow University/Oxford University/ London Scottish. Indian Civil Service/ Major in RAF. 7 caps for Scotland (1905-08).

Frederick Mark (Tim) TAYLOR Fly half. Born Leicester 18/3/1888. Died Evington, Leicester 2/3/1966. 1 cap for England (1914). Medway Street School, Leicester/ Medway Old Boys/Medway Athletic/Leicester/ Midland Counties/Leicestershire. Brother Frank won 2 caps (1920). Lieutenant in RAF, then solicitors' clerk.

John Lyon HAMILTON Scrum half, later wing. Born 20/12/1892. Captain in RAF.

William Wavell (Wakers) WAKEFIELD (later Lord Wakefield) Forward. Born Beckenham 10/3/1898. Died aged 85, Kendal, 12/8/1983. Craig Prep. School/Sedbergh School/Cambridge University/Neath/Leicester/ Harlequins/Middlesex. 31 caps for England (1920-27), very influential in the game. Pilot/politician/company director. Began in the Royal Naval Air Service before becoming a Pilot in the new RAF. Flying-Officer then Flight-Lieutenant in the RAF. A Member of Parliament, with breaks, 1935-63. Was President of the RFU, 1950-51. He was created Baron Wakefield of Kendal.

George THOM Forward. Born Gateshead 13/3/1890. Died British Columbia (Canada) August 1927. Kirkcaldy High School/Kirkcaldy. Scotland 4 caps (1920). Captain in the RAF. Uncle of J R Thom who won 3 caps (1933).

Robert Sturley SIMPSON Forward. Born Kinning Park, Glasgow 28/4/1899. Died Wincanton 16/1/1991 (aged 91). Loretto School/Glasgow Academy/Glasgow Academicals. Scotland 1 cap (1923). Lieutenant.

Abraham Hugo MALAN Forward. South African. Lieutenant in the British Expeditionary Force in France. Played for the North-West Area (RAF).

Edward F TURNER Forward. London Scottish. Captain, later Flight-Lieutenant. Possibly Edward Fisher Turner, born 12/10/1895.

Jack P FINDLAY Forward. Captain in RAF, 'mystery man' with initials listed as JP, JT, TP and EF! Wakefield writes of TP, but JP is more likely, Ira Jones calling him 'Jack Findlay from the Cape'. He played for Western Province (Town & Country) v the 1924 GB team.

Hjalmar Harison (Harry) THESEN Forward. Second-Lieut. Born Knysna, SA of Norwegian descent, 23/12/1889. Part of Thesen & Co., shipping. Died Knysna 4/6/1961. Married Edna Reid, 3 children.

'Harry' Thesen

Sadly missed at hs S African home

Richard Burnard MUNDAY, DSC, AFC, Belgian Croix de Guerre Forward. Born Plumpton, Devon 31/1/1896, died 11/7/1932. Nine kills as a Squadron-Leader in No 8 Naval Squadron, RNAS. Wounded 1916, but continued. Later a Major. Married in Brussels 1930. Epsom College/Guy's Hospital.

Additionally, for the game v South Africa:

James Hart MITCHELL, MC, DFC Wing/Full back. Captain in the 28th Squadron, RAF. Munster/Public Schools XV. Born Hereford 8/5/1899. Died Dorset 1974. Awarded the Military Cross 1918, the Distinguished Flying Cross and Italy's Bronze Medal for military valour. 18 kills. Resigned his commission in 1921.

James Mitchell

Gerard Bruce CROLE, MC Wing. Born Edinburgh 7/6/1894. Died Aberdeen 31/3/1965. Edinburgh Academy/Oxford University (Blue 1913). Scotland 4 caps (1920) 3 tries. 2nd Lt., then Capt. Dragoon

Guards and RFA, and Flight Commander 40 & 43 Squadrons, Royal Flying Corps: 5 credited victories. Prisoner of War. MC in 1917. Sudan political service/schoolmaster/solicitor. Scotland cricketer. For Scotland *v* England in 1920, he marked Cyril Lowe, who was credited with nine aerial victories: the only occasion when two fighter aces were directly opposed in a rugby test?

R C THOMAS Fly half. Major. Not known if he was a Welshman!

Archibald William (Archie) SYMINGTON, MC Forward. Born Calcutta, India, March 1892. Died North Connel, Argyllshire 8/5/1941 (a long way from his home, Allanton, Dumfries). Fettes College/London Scottish/Cambridge University (3 Blues 1911-13). Scotland 2 caps (1914). Lieutenant, Royal Kings Rifle Corps then Flying Officer in the Royal Flying Corps. Wounded at Bethune in December 1914. Military Cross in 1916. Bankrupt 1933.

Additionally, for the game v the Mother Country:

Herbert Wilfred (Herbie) TAYLOR, MC Fly half. Born Durban 5/5/1889. Died Newlands, Cape Town 8/2/1973. Lieutenant in the Royal Field Artillery, then the Royal Flying Corps. He gained the Military Cross. He was an outstanding South African cricketer, captaining his country and playing in 42 tests (1912-1932), scoring 2,936 runs and taking 156 wickets. He was Natal's rugby fly-half from about 1909 through to at least 1921, having started playing club rugby with the Durban Rovers (effectively a Michaelhouse School Old Boys team), steering them to the Murray Cup in the Natal clubs championship in 1909, and was Natal's fly-half twice against the 1910 GB side. He was a Blackheath centre/ fly half in 1919 and 1920. He could not tour with 1912-13 Springboks to GB/France, as he was needed by the South African cricket side in England in 1912 for Triangular Test series with Australia. His elder brother, Daniel, also played against GB in 1910 as a wing and played test cricket for South Africa.

A H M COPELAND Forward. Captain in the RAF. Believed to be **Arthur H M COPELAND** a Canadian, born Winnipeg 27/8/1889, went to Milton District School. Died 18/10/1984 at Milton, nr. Toronto, aged 95. Signed up in Winnipeg and joined 25th Squadron RFC. An observer/navigator in the ASC/RFC, his plane was shot down and the pilot killed. A PoW in Germany until January 1919. Later owned a wholesale materials firm, Copeland Lumber.

Additionally, for the game v Australia:

William Francis WARNER Wing. Lieutenant.

L RENDLES Lieutenant. South African. Played for Natal against GB in 1910.

William Henry GREER Forward. Had been a Captain in the RNAC.

Harry BATES, MM Forward. Lieutenant. Military Medal. South-West Area (RAF)

Additionally, for the game v Canada:

W G CLARKE Centre. Lieutenant. May have been a South African.

C W THOMPSON Forward. Captain in RAF.

The following RAF men from the King's Cup played in post-war Inter-Service Tournaments:

J I T Jones - vs Navy 1920; Navy, Army 1921, 1922.

W W Wakefield - vs Navy, Army 1920, 1921, 1922, 1923 (all as captain).

E F Turner - vs Navy 1920; Navy, Army 1921, 1922, 1925; Navy 1926, 1927.

4.7   SOUTH AFRICA

The Springboks, as the South African teams had become known before the war, were to develop into one of the greatest rugby powers.

Their rivalry with New Zealand, in particular, was for much of the 20th century to be the major power struggle in the world game, though their first official international meeting did not occur until 1921.

The All Blacks were to prevail, 13-5, in Dunedin, but the three match series was drawn.

So their game during this King's Cup series was probably the most significant clash to that date between representatives of two countries who were to become rugby rivals on a huge, sometimes bitter and often controversial scale.

In 1902, just 12 years before the Great War began, the armies of Britain and the Boer Republics in South Africa (Transvaal and Orange Free State) had been fighting each other in the Second Boer War.

There had been an extraordinary transformation in relationships between the countries in the intervening period and despite some continued opposition there, the Union of South Africa was to prove Britain's staunch and hard-fighting ally after 1914.

South African units fought on three fronts: nearest home, in German South-West Africa; in the wide-ranging conflict in East Africa and of course in France, to which an infantry brigade and various other units moved.

In addition, it is estimated that about 3,000 South Africans joined the Royal Flying Corps, later the RAF. Total South African war casualties reached 18,600, with more than 6,600 losing their lives, some 5,000 of those on the Western Front.

It was the survivors there who provided the pool of rugby players from which these represented their homeland in the King's Cup:

In their first game, v the RAF:

> **A W F ROPER, MC** Full back. Captain in South African Army, Heavy Artillery. Military Cross. Lived in Rhodesia.

Walter James (Wally) MILLS Wing. Born Durbanville 16/6/1891. Died Somerset West (SA) 23/2/1975. Hamilton (Sea Point) RFC/ Stellenbosch University/Western Province. 1 cap (1910). Toured with South Africa to GB in 1912-13. Lieutenant. Played for Western Province Colleges and for Cape Colony against the tourists in 1910.

T H MILLS Centre. Captain, South African Army. Played for Transvaal v GB in 1910.

D V SCULLY Centre. Second-Lieutenant, 2nd South African Infantry.

Stanley Wakefield (Stan) HARRIS, CBE Wing. Born Somerset East 13/12/1893. Died Kenilworth, Cape Town 3/10/1973. Bedford School/Blackheath/East Midlands/Pirates RFC (SA)/Kenya/Transvaal/ GB. England 2 caps

W J 'Wally' Mills

(1920). GB to SA 1924 (2 tests). Began as a Gunnery Lieutenant in the South African Army. Badly wounded at the Somme. Reached finals of World Amateur Ballroom Championships, winning the waltz! A Wimbledon tennis doubles winner, he represented England at polo, but turned down a chance of representing Great Britain at modern pentathlon in the 1930 Olympics. South African light-heavyweight boxing champion in 1921 and played Davis Cup tennis doubles for SA. Member of the Army Sports Control Board 1935-1939. In WW2 he became a prisoner of war of the Japanese in Singapore and Siam for 3½ years, being promoted to Lieutenant-Colonel and commanding officer of the Bedfordshire Yeomanry in captivity. Awarded the CBE in 1946. Had a silver plate in his hip.

V St G LEGER Fly half. Bombardier.

William Henry (Taffy) TOWNSEND Scrum half. Born 12/3/1896, Newport, Wales. Killed in action, WW2, Catania, Sicily 27/1/1943. 1 cap (1921). Old Collegians/Natal. Private, then Corporal in the SA Infantry. Diamond digger.

William Henry (Boy) MORKEL Forward, from one of the most famous of SA rugby families. Born Somerset West 2/1/1886 (or 1885).

Died Worcester, Cape Province 6/2/1955. Diggers RFC/Western Province. 9 caps (1910-21), three as captain. Toured with South Africa to GB in 1912-13 and to Australia/New Zealand in 1921. Farmer. Several brothers and other family members were also capped. He was a Captain in the South African Army.

Wilhelm August George (Bingo) BURGER Forward. Born Hamburg, Cape Province 12/8/1883. Died Alice, Ciskei 8/8/1963. Albert RFC/Border. 4 caps (1906-10). South African tour to GB in 1906-07. Sergeant.

Listed as E RIORDEN, but was probably: **Clifford Atherton (Cliff) RIORDEN** Forward. Born Colesberg 24/12/1885. Died London 7/2/1958. Diggers RFC/Transvaal. 2 caps (1910). Gunner in the South African Infantry.

'Bingo' Burger: a new fast food?

Listed as G Mellish but was actually **Frank Whitmore MELLISH, MC** – Forward. Born Rondebosch, Western Province 26/3(or 4)/1897. Died in Cape Town 21/8/1965. Wynberg Boys High School/Rondebosch Boys High School/South African College School/Cape Town Highlanders/Villagers RFC/Blackheath/ Barbarians/Western Province. England 6 caps (1920-21). South Africa 6 caps (1921-24). South Africa tour to Australia/New Zealand 1921. Manager, South African tour to GB/France in 1951-52. Gunner in the Cape Town Highlanders/ then Lieutenant in the South African Heavy Artillery, being wounded in a leg in 1918. Awarded the Military Cross in 1916 at Ypres. In WW2 he was a Colonel in the South African Armoured Division. Business executive with United Tobacco Company and a flower farmer.

Frank Mellish 1951

A O L BROWNLEE Forward. Captain in the South African Forces (Medical).

F A BENNETTO Forward. Corporal in the South African Forces. Kimberley Boys High School/Griqualand West (played v GB tourists in 1924).

H Walter STOCKDALE, DFC Forward. Born Pietermaritzburg. Died Natal 25/10/1928. Captain in the South African Forces/Wing Commander Flying Corps (101 Squadron). Maritzburg College (cricket captain 1912). Awarded the Star of Romania 1919. In WW2 had Richard Dimbleby on board as an observer in a 1944 raid.

J SCHWARTZ Forward. Private in the South African Forces.

Additionally, for the game v Australia

W STOLL Full back. Lieutenant.

G (or C) M GLENCROSS Forward. Public School Services XV/Blenheim. Sergeant.

Additionally, for the game v Canada:

Benjamin Frederick (Fred) WINDELL Full back, later fly half. Private in the First Battalion, South African Infantry. Played fly half twice for Orange Free State against GB in 1924.

N CARBATT (or CARBUTT) Forward. Captain.

M VERSFIELD Forward. Second Lieutenant. Western Province.

A H MILLER Forward. Lieutenant.

V J SCHOLTZ Forward. Gunner.

Additionally, for the game v New Zealand:

Lieutenant D DUNCAN Forward

Cadet D A St J WOLFE Forward

Additionally, for the game v the Mother Country:

I B D de VILLIERS Full back. Sergeant. He starred for Witwatersrand against the GB tourists of 1924, scoring two penalties and a dropped goal in the 10-6 win in Johannesburg.

5

The Tournament

"...Ending with the biggest game in the history of Rugby, against an All British team, composed of all internationals from England, Scotland, Wales, and Ireland"

MATCH 1:
New Zealand v Royal Air Force
22-3

MARCH 1ST 1919   **ST. HELEN'S, SWANSEA**

Unfortunately, the RAF lost three of their best players when illness struck en route to Wales. In any event, they had not had much time together, while New Zealand were not only at full strength, but were a tried and tested unit for this St David's Day tournament opener at a Swansea ground well used to hosting major internationals.

As 'Wakers' put it, '...*influenza raged and destroyed our prospects of getting together a reasonable team in time for our first match and we were badly beaten by the New Zealanders at Swansea on my first visit to that ground.*'

Reports suggested that no better venue could have been chosen for the first match in the Cup, as Swansea was a town rich in rugby tradition and memories. A crowd of around 10,000 was expected, but in fact only some 2,500 turned up and it was suggested that 'Taffy' (the regular Welsh supporter) had no personal interest in the players of either side. The attendance was indeed much smaller than it might have been, but this was probably due in the most part to so many people refusing to pay the increased gate charges. Also, many understandably considered the result was a foregone conclusion.

In the event, New Zealand were tested far harder than was expected and it was rather closer than the final score suggested. The big surprise was the way the RAF pack tore into their opponents, with their dribbling being a feature of the game, but New Zealand were more skillful out wide, while Charlie Brown and Jack McNaught were quick in their decisions.

Despite playing into the strong wind it was 6-0 at half-time to New Zealand, led by capped scrum half Charles Brown, with wing Percy Storey having crossed twice from brilliant passing, despite missing two other chances, and 'Jockey' Ford was notable for his clever cross-kicking. The RAF went close twice.

Charlie Brown's NZ Cap

After the restart a rapid burst by 'Ranji' Wilson sent Storey in for his hat-trick, but at 9-0 and into

St. Helen's Ground, Swansea

the breeze there came the best try of the match, scored by Tennant Sloan for the airmen, as he left the steady New Zealand full back Capper completely fooled and unable to tackle him.

The RAF pressed strongly, but suddenly New Zealand upped a gear and it was all over as further tries followed in quick succession from Jack Stohr, Bill Fea and 'Moke' Belliss, two of them being converted, probably by Stohr, though one report suggested it was the forward Sellars who had taken over the goalkicking after Stohr had missed the first three conversions.

The RAF included the South African George Wrentmore as centre and captain, and the then-uncapped Wavell Wakefield up front. At that time, of course, a try and a penalty were equally valued at three points, with a dropped goal worth four.

That wind played a big part as passes went astray, but it was a good opener in the Principality, where only one of the game's 30 players was Welsh. Winger Jones, could have had a try in the first half, but Wrentmore held on and was tackled.

Godfrey Wentmore, RAF Skipper

Much missed

An interesting story surrounds the identity of that last-minute replacement wing, who turns out to have been Captain J Ira T 'Taffy' Jones, born a little further west of Swansea: he of No. 74 'Tiger' Squadron fame, the highest-scoring Welsh fighter ace – in the air, rather than the on-pitch battles!

According to his autobiographical *An Air Fighter's Scrapbook*, with its lovingly-detailed chapter on his rugby exploits, Ira Jones had meant to attend the match merely as a spectator, but was talked into taking the field to replace yet another sick player, a winger named Gustav Adolph Eugene Norgarb, a South African from Pretoria, who on January 15, 1918 had risen from Lieutenant to Captain. Norgarb had played in the first-ever RAF match a month earlier and at centre inside him in that match was his younger brother, John Hermann Carstens Norgarb, who had also been promoted to Captain.

It was Gustav, aged 27, who had to withdraw at the very last moment at Swansea, with Jones luckily on hand to play. The Wanganui Chronicle kept Norgarb in its team lineups, yet referred to the lack of ball that went the way of his replacement Jones! Neither of the Norgarb brothers played in the Cup: Gustav married a lady from Kensington in 1920, though she was to return from S Africa after a decade to marry a Yorkshire ship engineer.

Meanwhile, while stand-in Jones was not called upon again in the tournament, he did appear in the Inter-Service Tournament against the Royal Navy in 1920, 1921 and 1922 and the Army in 1921 and 1922.

Other late RAF changes had seen full back Captain James Mitchell, South African fly half Lieutenant Randles and Lieutenant C Lawton Ross, a forward, all miss out.

This game saw Wakefield's introduction to major representative rugby. An excellent all-round athlete, he helped revolutionise the role of the back row forward, his athleticism enabled him to play a more dynamic role: pressuring half backs in defence and supporting the threequarters' attacks, the prime responsibilities of the modern open side. A complete footballer, he had all the attributes – strength, weight and speed – of a great forward. A master of dribbling with pace, he was aggressive, up with his backs in attack, took and gave passes well, and seemed a born leader.

New Zealand – +C H Capper; +W A Ford, *L B Stohr, +P W Storey; G J McNaught, +W R Fea; *C Brown (capt); A P Singe, *E W Hasell, R Sellars, E L J Cockcroft, *N A Wilson, J Kissick, +E A Belliss, +R Fogarty.

Tries – Storey 3, Stohr, Fea, Belliss. Cons – Stohr (?) or Sellars 2.

RAF – W Seddon (RL); Captain J I T Jones, G M Wrentmore (capt), C D (may be E N) Fuller, *L H T Sloan; *F M Taylor, J L Hamilton; +W W Wakefield, +G Thom, +R S Simpson, A H Malan, E F Turner, J P Findlay, H H Thesen, R B Munday.

Try – Sloan.

(* – denotes capped before the war; + – capped or played for a NZ XV after the war; RL – rugby league)

Referee – not known.

MATCH 2:
Mother Country v Australia
6-3

MARCH 8th 1919   **WELFORD RD, LEICESTER**

The Mother Country side (called the Home Countries in the programme for this clash in the East Midlands, at Leicester) were all Army men and every one an officer. Eight English caps (before or after), two each from Wales and Scotland and one Irish were in the XV, with only wing Charles Pantlin (Irish triallist) and Glasgow Academicals hooker Bill Findlay failing to gain one.

They lost forward Alex Sykes with a bad nose injury for almost all of a rough game. There were many wrestling-style melees, but Aussie full back Jackie Beith was outstanding in an even contest, while the home side looked ring-rusty.

Australia were in some respects unlucky, as they spent much of the match in the Mother Country half and won the scrummage duels; their opponents looked tired at times and critics were left thinking that the home side contained too many officers.

F. & J. SMITH'S CIGARETTES

CARDIFF, R.F.C.
C. LEWIS,
O.H.M.S.

Try scorer Clem Lewis

It was not really a game for spectators, being rather too much like the wrong sort of a cup-tie: a tight struggle, as Australia mostly took it to the Mother Country up front.

It was nearly half-time before the Mother Country backs got a chance to show their skills and when John Pym made a break, Reg Pickles carried it on and sent the little Wales fly half Clem Lewis over for a try.

The threes were where Mother Country was at its best as Pickles, Day and Cullen were all keen to put back their heads and run hard for the line.

In the second half the Mother Country attacked but Beith stood firm, fielding and tackling resolutely and halting efforts by Day and 'Cherry' Pillman.

Australia came back into it as 'Rat' Flanagan at scrum half sniped on the blind-side before the men from Down Under snatched a try by wing Tom Stenning to level the scores, and it looked as if the Mother Country might suffer defeat in their first tournament outing.

However, home full back Barry Cumberlege (who was to gain his first England cap in 1920) then hit the post with a penalty before kicking the winner in the final minute of the battle.

At that stage it was not expected that the Mother Country would worry New Zealand, but they were getting fitter by the day and were to astound some of their critics.

Incidentally, the Mother Country half backs on the day had opposed each other at Twickenham in 1912, when both were winning their first caps. Pym partnered Adrian Stoop and Lewis had Dickie Owen as his scrum half, when England beat Wales 8-0.

'Darb' Hickey

Mother Country – +B S Cumberlege; +H L V Day, +W J Cullen, +R C W Pickles, C W R Pantlin; *+J C M Lewis, *J A Pym; *+C M Usher, *J S Brunton, *C H Pillman, *A R V Sykes, *+L G Brown, +Rev W T Havard, W G K Findlay, +R A Gallie.

Try – Lewis. **Pen** – Cumberlege.

Australia – *+B M Beith; *D C Suttor, *D Hickey, T R Stenning; +P N Buchanan, J C Watkins, T W Flanagan; *W T Watson (capt), *+J H Bond, A M Lyons, *E A S Cody, W R Bradley, *J Thompson, J Murray, G E See.

Try – Stenning.

Referee – Not known.

MATCH 3:
South Africa v Royal Air Force
12-0

MARCH 8th 1919   **TWICKENHAM**

The RAF, playing their second match, held South Africa at forward but were beaten out wide on a day when Twickenham was being used for only the second time since 1914. Despite being played in heavy rain it was a good match, pleasing to watch, and while the running was impressive, the tackling on both sides was even better.

Overall, the tournament was starting to grow on the rugby public, with good forward play by all sides to date. With backs willing to run and use the ball that made for more exciting games.

Stan Harris, an astonishing all-round sportsman, was quite outstanding as a wing for South Africa. He was later to become an England international, a British tourist back to South Africa at rugby, and much more else besides.

Major R C Thomas, at fly half, was the best RAF back and Scotland's George Thom (capped the following year) was the best forward on the field.

In those days long, long before substitutes, the RAF lost Scotland international Archie Symington, who was injured in the second half, but his side was already 12 points behind.

Scot George Thom

It was the first real test for the Twickenham pitch since 1914 and the ground was in good condition to start, though the rain made it trickier as the game went on.

Billy Seddon was a typical rugby league full back of those days – a rock in defence and solid in his touch-kicking.

Harris scored the first try in great style after leaving three defenders in his wake, handing-off the third, before scoring with a full-length dive to the line as he was tackled He became a marked man, but somehow the other South African backs were not able to capitalise on the extra space they were given.

Scully in the centre had dropped the ball on several occasions, but then redeemed himself by adding a clever dropped goal to stretch the lead.

Finally, from the South African point of view, the Newport-born scrum half 'Taffy' Townsend scrambled over after his forwards had driven to the line and Scully converted.

There was no reply, for although the RAF forward George Thom dribbled splendidly he fell as he came close to the line. Thom had a fine game, and though aged 30 and uncapped, his form was to attract the Scotland selectors sufficiently to cap him in all four Championship matches of 1920. He emigrated to Canada and died there at the age of 38.

'Wakers' wrote of this clash: '... *I played my first match at Twickenham, against the South Africans, when, with a still depleted team, we were beaten 12-0. I remember being greatly impressed by the size of the South African forwards, and the difficulty of getting the ball in the line-out...*'

Welsh-born 'Taffy' Townsend of SA

South Africa – A W Roper; *W J Mills, T H Mills, D V Scully, +S W Harris; V St G Leger; +W H Townsend; *+W H Morkel (capt), *W A Burger, *C A Riorden, +F W Mellish, A O Brownlee, F A Bennetto, H W Stockdale, J Schwartz.

Tries – Harris, Townsend. **Con** – Scully. **DG** – Scully.

RAF – W Seddon (RL); J Mitchell, G M Wrentmore (capt), *L H T Sloan, +G B Crole; R C Thomas, J L Hamilton; +W W Wakefield, +G Thom, +R S Simpson, *A W Symington, A H Malan, E F Turner, H H Thesen, J P Findlay.

Referee – Frank C Potter-Irwin (England). Ilford Wanderers RFC. Vice-president of the RFU. Refereed eight internationals (1909-20), plus six Varsity matches. Died in 1957, aged 77.

MATCH 4:
New Zealand v Canada
11-0

MARCH 8th 1919   **PORTSMOUTH**

At the United Services Club ground, Portsmouth, New Zealand fielded a side composed almost entirely of reserves. That day, as we have seen, their first team was defeating Yorkshire at Lidget Green, Bradford. Perhaps encouraged, Canada put in a fine effort, doing so even without their centre, Almond Grimmett, who was off the field injured for most of the first half before gallantly returning after the interval.

Holland at full back was a defiant last line of defence, but with his forwards outgunned there was little hope as New Zealand kept attacking, doing enough to win, yet never totally overwhelming their game opponents.

Canada looked like a side that had been together very little and most of them were more used to American football, but they worked hard and had plenty of energy, which would hopefully see them improve as the tournament continued.

In the opening minutes, NZ scrum half Don Sandman sold a dummy and went over and Dick Roberts converted. Centre Ed Ryan, one of 13 of his side making their debut in the competition, then raced away for a superb individual try to make it 8-0 at half-time.

United Services Ground, Portsmouth

It was Ryan who scored the only points of the second spell. With a fine effort, he again capped a clever run by bursting over for his second try, but surprisingly there was no further score and the Canadians contributed some good individual moments of their own.

This was a game in which New Zealand took a calculated risk in sending their best 15 players to Bradford and hoping that their next best 15 could beat the weakest team in the competition.

Only a month earlier Canada had held New Zealand's 'Reserves' to 12-0 at Chiswick in a match where Canada had tackled splendidly. The New Zealand backs had fallen away from their usual form and for the greater part were proven to be ordinary, yet still in the end the 'smarter' side.

However, the gamble was taken at Portsmouth, and it paid off with a win, albeit not a big one.

New Zealand – +C H Capper; W L Henry, E Ryan, G L Owles; *E R W Roberts, E Watson; D Mc K Sandman; *M J Cain, S J Standen, E J Naylor, A Gilchrist, F P Arnold, C W Tepene, A A Lucas, +R Fogarty.

Tries – Ryan 2, Sandman. **Con** – Roberts.

Canada – Corporal F Holland; Sapper J H Pritchard, Lieutenant E W W Watling, Captain A M Grimmett, Corporal J D Phillips; Lance-Corporal G Edwards (capt), Lieutenant C C Kenning; Private M A Hall, Sergeant F A Herman, Quartermaster-Sergeant/Major J C Shine, Sergeant F Dobbs, Lieutenant R Wilson, Private H A Brennan, Quartermaster-Sergeant/Major H Yeoman, Major H D Deedes.

Referee – Not known.

MATCH 5:
Australia v South Africa
8-5

MARCH 15th 1919   RODNEY PARADE, NEWPORT

It was back to Wales, this time at Newport for a mighty battle between two evenly-matched sides. A draw might have been a fairer result, and it was hard to believe then that neither side was to feature in the eventual play-off match.

Wally Matthews in action

Centre T H Mills was unable to play for South Africa and worse still for them, the great 'Boy' Morkel was ill with influenza, but Australia also had problems as their outstanding wing, Tom Stenning, was forced to retire with injury for a spell. Although he came back on, he eventually had to leave for good: however he was able to play against Devon County a few weeks later.

Manager Wally Matthews had to turn out at fly half for Australia, who took the scrums while South Africa led at the line-out, but it was when the latter gained their first clean heel of the match that they were able to open the scoring.

The South African pack gained possession and fly half St Leger sent Wally Mills away. He transferred well to send across Roper, a winger who had previously played as full back, for a try that Scully converted.

However, Australia came back to give the new full back Stoll a hard time in defence, and their driving pack put the South Africans on the back foot, culminating in wing Dudley Suttor running in for a try before the interval.

Try scorer 'Dud' Suttor

An early image of Rodney Parade

South Africa still led by two points, but after the break Suttor got away again and if his first try was good, this was even better as he eluded several would-be tacklers before putting the supporting forward Bill Bradley in for the winning try, Stenning converting in his brief spell back on the field.

From then on it was nip and tuck, quite exciting for the most part but with Australia just on top in what had proved another fine advert for the sport and the tournament.

Australia – *+B M Beith; *D C Suttor, J H Bosward, H R Pountney, T R Stenning; W F Matthews, T W Flanagan; *W T Watson (capt), *+J H Bond, A M Lyons, *E A S Cody, W R Bradley, G E See, T Quinn, +V A Dunn.

Tries – Suttor, Bradley. **Con** – Stenning.

South Africa – W Stoll; A W Roper, *W J Mills, D V Scully, +S W Harris; V St G Leger; +W H Townsend; *W A Burger, *C A Riorden, +F W Mellish, G (or C) M Glencross, A O Brownlee, F A Bennetto, H W Stockdale, J Schwartz.

Try – (WJ) Mills. **Con** – Scully.

Referee – Not known.

MATCH 6:
Mother Country v RAF
29-6

MARCH 15th 1919   **TWICKENHAM**

Two players – one on each side – became most interesting debutants in the competition, which at this stage was still being called The Inter-Services and Dominions Championship by most members of the media.

Company Sergeant Major Charles Jones, later capped by Wales in 1920, became the first ever non-officer to play for both the Army and the Mother Country, while the great South African test cricket batsman, Herbie Taylor, played at fly half for the RAF. Second row Robert Sholto Hedderwick of London Scottish, then aged 32 and who was to remain uncapped, was now in the Mother Country pack. 'Cherry' Pillman, in the back row, had played twice for the 1910 GB tourists to South Africa against Taylor, who had then been in Durban, and, along with his brother, represented Natal.

Herbie Taylor

Despite earlier rain, the ground staff had worked hard to prepare a good pitch for what was, if somewhat one-sided at times, a delightful game to watch.

The Mother Country team's fitness and team play was steadily improving and although the RAF repulsed early attacks, a score had to come, albeit only by the clever boot of Clem Lewis, with a drop goal. It was the sole score of a half in which the opposing full backs – Billy Seddon and Barry Cumberlege – excelled.

'Cherry' Pillman

Scotland 1920 were to feature the RAF's Thom as well as our foursome from this 1919 match: Usher, Allen Sloan, Crole (RAF) & Gallie

Dribbling by forwards was then an art and the RAF certainly knew how to do it, but they met the talented 27-year-old Cumberlege and he dealt well with those forays. Wakefield again '... *against the Mother Country the one incident I vividly recall was the extraordinary speed with which Barry Cumberlege whipped the ball off my feet when I had gone away in a long dribble.*'

The full back was then uncapped, and had supposedly turned down the British tour invitation in 1910, while still aged 18 and at Durham School. He was 28 before winning the first of eight England caps and went on to referee 16 international matches.

In the second half tries started to flow freely from the Mother Country, Lewis working wing Harold Day over, then Day sending his centre Bill Cullen in with a return pass before Allen Sloan raced clear with a fine solo effort.

The RAF hit back with a good try by wing Gerard Crole, who was to be capped four times by Scotland in 1920 and who, soon after being awarded the Military Cross, had become a prisoner of war.

There was to be a further RAF score from 'Bai' Wrentmore's well-judged penalty, but it was the Mother Country, led by the intricate running of Lewis, which finished well on top.

This led to four more tries, two converted, with a pair by Sloan, to complete his hat-trick, while Brown and Pickles also crossed.

Most of the media concluded that, though it was another fine game, the limited opposition made it hard

The RAF's (later Sir) Tennant Sloan, Scotland 1905-08

to assess just how much progress that the Mother Country had made. Still, they had run in seven tries and only conceded one.

The programme from March 15th 1919

Mother Country – +B S Cumberlege; +H L V Day, +W J Cullen, +R C W Pickles, *+A T Sloan; *+J C M Lewis, *J A Pym; *+C M Usher, *J S Brunton, *C H Pillman, R S Hedderwick, *+L G Brown, +Rev W T Havard, +C W Jones, +R A Gallie.

Tries – Sloan 3, Brown, Day, Cullen, Pickles. **Cons** – Brown, Lewis. **DG** – Lewis.

RAF – W Seddon (RL); J Mitchell, G M Wrentmore (capt), *L H T Sloan, +G B Crole; H W Taylor, J L Hamilton; +W W Wakefield, +G Thom, +R S Simpson, A H M Copeland, A H Malan, E F Turner, H H Thesen, J P Findlay.

Try – Crole. **Pen** – Wrentmore.

Referee – Not known.

MATCH 7:
South Africa v Canada
31-0

MARCH 22nd 1919   **ST. HELEN'S, SWANSEA**

The third and final game in South Wales brought the competition back to the historic St Helen's Ground in Swansea, only a few yards from the seashore. It saw a very easy victory for South Africa, despite snow having fallen just before the kick-off to make conditions potentially tricky.

That didn't seem to hamper the South African attackers, as they ran in nine tries and two of their threequarters – both named Mills, but unrelated – ran riot with seven tries between them. Four fell to the more experienced W J 'Wally' Mills on the wing, while centre T H Mills had to be content with a hat-trick.

Centre Scully and scrum half 'Taffy' Townsend were the others to touch down, but only two of the tries were converted, sparing the brave losers from a still larger margin.

From a land with so much less big-game experience – their 1902 tour of Britain, with an all-British Columbian side and no Test matches, was a smaller, pioneering venture compared with the Springboks' 1906 and 1912 visits – the Canadians again tried hard, but for the second successive match did not trouble the scoreboard.

The game was not of a great standard, with South Africa not at their best. They didn't really need to be, though, as Canada again showed their lack of knowledge of tactics and, at times, of the rules of rugby union. It was probably their worst performance of the tournament.

Several of the Canadian squad seem to have been comparatively recent emigrants from Britain, and the English-born pair of Richardson on the wing and Hall in the pack both worked hard for the losers, while the other wing, Pritchard, got through a lot of the very-necessary defensive duty.

South Africa – B F Windell; *W J Mills, T H Mills, D V Scully, +S W Harris; V St G Leger; +W H Townsend;*C A Riorden, +F W Mellish, A O Brownlee (capt), F A Bennetto, N Carbatt, M Versfield, A H Miller, V J Scholtz.

Tries – (WJ) Mills 4, (TH) Mills 3, Townsend, Scully. **Cons** – Scully, Townsend.

Canada – F Holland; J H Pritchard, E W W Watling, A Vickery, S B Richardson; G Edwards (capt), C C Kenning; M A Hall, F A Herman, R Wilson, H E Brennan, H J McDonald, T McQuarrie, J C Wakefield, H F McGuingan.

Referee – Not known.

MATCH 8:
Mother Country v Canada
22-0

MARCH 29th 1919   **INVERLEITH**

It had been announced three days before this match that King George V would present 'The King's Cup' to the tournament's winning team, and after this clash it became more common for that to be the media's title of choice for the competition. To date, royalty had not watched any of the games. However, that was all to change.

On the field, though, Canada failed to score for the third time in 22 days, and they conceded six tries: the Mother Country, however, managed only two conversions.

Four players made their debuts for Canada while the Mother Country brought in both the pre-War Scotland cap, 'Podger' Laing, who went on to play for his country until 1921, and the very fine uncapped forward Major Peter Lawless, who earned the Military Cross in WW1 and was to die in WW2 at the age of 45. Captain Usher was one who was not able to make the trip up to Scotland.

The Mother Country were not only getting fitter but also looking more like a side, rather than a group of good individual players. Again, they had far too much experience for their opponents.

Both John Pym and Clem Lewis at half-back had been wounded during their Army service, but they were in fine form to launch a fast set of threequarters. They got off to a great start, with Bill Cullen soon across the line and then, when centre Reg Pickles was halted just short, Pym popped up to gather and score.

Cullen made the next try for wing Allen Sloan and then Pym was over again, though the wind was too strong for the conversion efforts of Barry Cumberlege (three times) and Lewis.

Canada still had to make do with players to whom rugby union was a relatively unknown sport, but they improved as the game went on with the forwards making a great effort with the wind in the second half.

'Podger' Laing

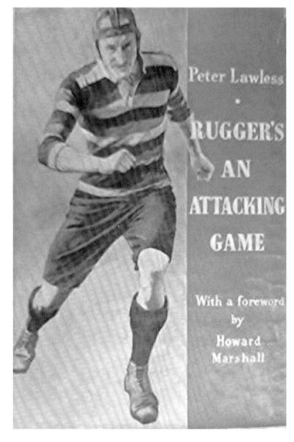

Lawless, fell in WW2   *His posthumous book*

It was also probably fair to conclude that the Mother Country eased off to an extent with the match effectively won. However, in the final quarter Lewis began a move that saw Pickles score, before 'Cherry' Pillman gained the final try from a close-range scrum, with Lewis placing both conversions.

The Queen's Own Cameron Highlanders played the music before the match at this Edinburgh ground where Scotland were to play their home games until 1925, and the referee for this clash, unlike many of the others, was very well known!

Mother Country – +B S Cumberlege; +H L V Day, +W J Cullen, +R C W Pickles, *+A T Sloan; *+J C M Lewis (capt), *J A Pym; *J S Brunton, *C H Pillman, *+L G Brown, +Rev W T Havard, *+A D Laing, P H Lawless, +C W Jones, +R A Gallie.

Tries – Pym 2, Cullen, Sloan, Pickles, Pillman. **Cons** – Lewis 2.

Canada – Private Evans; C H Perry, J Holland, A M Grimmett, J D Phillips; G Edwards (capt), E J Hellings; M A Hall, F A Herman, J C Shine, F Dobbs, R Wilson, Sergeant-Major Guthrie, H Yeoman, H J McDonald.

Referee – John Dewar Dallas (Scotland) – Born 1878. Died Aberdeen 31/7/1942. Played for George Watson's College/Watsonians. Refereed Wales v NZ 1905, disallowing the Bob Deans 'try'. 1 cap for Scotland 1903. Aged 41 at the time of this match. He was a Sheriff and President of the Scottish RU 1912-13.

MATCH 9:
Royal Air Force v Australia
7-3

MARCH 29th 1919　　　　**KINGSHOLM, GLOUCESTER**

This match was originally due to be played at Plymouth, but was switched to Gloucester and produced an outstanding win for the RAF, defying the form book against a very good Australian team. However, as at Swansea, many local people refused to pay the increased gate charges.

At half-time Australia not only led 3-0, but were right on top both fore and aft and they should have increased their lead – but made some costly handling errors.

Two outstanding full backs – Billy Seddon and Jackie Beith – showed their class but the RAF somehow hung on, with the rugby league man Seddon rescuing them more than once.

Australia had the better pack and halves at that stage, but just one try early in the half by the fine front rower and highly decorated soldier, Bill Watson. He had been born in New Zealand, then, when he was 24, the family moved to Sydney. Bill had toured America and New Zealand pre-war with Australia and was now the captain.

He was a big, amiable man, unfortunately covered in festering sores from mustard gas attacks on the Western Front. He later married a lady from Victoria, gained three more caps and became a major in WW2. He was to be Australia's vice-consul in New York and died there after a very full life.

Australia's day at Gloucester was ruined, though, Seddon dropping a superb goal to put the RAF ahead by 4-3 and then the South African Godfrey Wrentmore placed an excellent long penalty to increase the lead.

Australia had two fine wings in Dudley Suttor and the newcomer, 'Pat' Egan, though another new man, Lieutenant Warner, and the former

Bill Watson, leader of men, here in WW2

PoW Gerrard Crole, in particular, kept them in close check. Egan played because Tom Stenning was injured.

It was an exciting game, but not of a high standard, as on numerous occasions the RAF had to hang on and scramble the ball away, while Australia, unusually for them, fumbled the ball far too often.

As well as Wrentmore, the RAF had other South African backs in Taylor and Rendles and that pair chose to keep the game tight despite having the dangerous Crole on the wing. Australia suffered in the same way as they also often chose not to bring their dangerous wingmen into action.

Wakefield was happier with this showing, of course: '*...when the effects of influenza wore off and we were able to put a full side into the field, we settled down into a good combination, and we managed to beat Australia at Gloucester, though they were in the running for the championship...*'

RAF – W Seddon (RL); W F Warner, G M Wrentmore (capt), *L H T Sloan, +G B Crole; H W Taylor, L Rendles; +W W Wakefield, +G Thom, +R S Simpson, A H Malan, E F Turner, H H Thesen, W H Greer, H Bates.

Pen – Wrentmore. **DG** – Seddon.

Australia – *+B M Beith; *D C Suttor, J H Boswood, H R Pountney, M (Pat) Egan; S Ryan, T W Flanagan; *W T Watson (capt), *+J H Bond, A M Lyons, W R Bradley, G E See, *J Thompson, J Murray, +V A Dunn.

Try – Watson.

Referee – Not known.

MATCH 10:
New Zealand v South Africa
14-5

MARCH 29th 1919   **TWICKENHAM**

This very first clash, at anything like top level, in what was to become rugby's most powerful, exciting and controversial rivalry was much awaited and did not disappoint. It inspired the tour of South Africa by the New Zealand team on their way home and set the trend and the tone for almost a century of future matches between these southern hemisphere giants. Within two years their first Test encounters had taken place, made the more likely and the more significant by this 1919 tournament and the strength of the Forces XVs which each nation was able to field. It provided a fitting overture for the duo's dramatic duels on the greater stages ahead.

A crowd of around 10,000 watched the finest game thus far, played in good weather and with the pitch in perfect condition. The match did not kick-off until 3.30pm, despite there being no floodlights then, and the many soldiers in the enclosures helped to create a great atmosphere, as did the intense tackling of both sides.

New Zealand brought in full back Jack O'Brien and he was fearless in defence, with the safest pair of hands of any player in the tournament's six sides.

The fitness of all the players was very noticeable, even after their recent efforts on other foreign fields, and although New Zealand won well in the end, they led only 6-5 against the run of play in the opening half, when South Africa had the wind at their backs.

Though they were playing well, South Africa went behind after 15 minutes when two defenders were troubled by a kick ahead and in the chase to the line it was the All Blacks' 22-year-old wing Percy Storey who won the touchdown.

South Africa hit back with a lovely try, made by quick passing. Scrum half 'Taffy' Townsend sent it out, fly half St Leger passing on to Wally Mills, now back on the wing, who got over for the try. Centre Scully converted.

The Army 'Boks' under powerful 'Boy' Morkel had another go and Stan Harris, soon to be capped by England, was tackled just short by O'Brien before New Zealand raced down to the other end and their new star, wing 'Jockey' Ford, was over to regain a lead of just one point at half-time.

The New Zealand forwards and the clever tactical kicking of O'Brien and Jack Stohr now pegged their opponents back, but South Africa tackled like demons. The All Blacks went back to their powerful pack, though, and both 'Nut' Hasell and 'Moke' Belliss crossed. Stohr, who was soon to emigrate to South Africa, converted the latter.

It was the pace of the back row forwards 'Ranji' Wilson and Singe that proved the ace card for New Zealand, as they handled as well as any back and their efforts led to both the second-half tries.

South Africa put together neat passing moves, yet New Zealand were always one step ahead and Sporting Life called it: *"... a hard, clean fight from beginning to end, which afforded an excellent afternoon's sport for a large and enthusiastic crowd."*

'Boy' Morkel: some boy!

Popular 'Baines of Bradford' Collectors' Shield

The Morning Post said: *"In the second half it did not take long to make out that the All Blacks were going to win. Their forwards played with that extra 'go' that always smacks of victory. As quick followers-up they are unsurpassed and in their splendid opportunism they continually looked like scorers."*

The Daily Telegraph commented: *"It was rugby with blood and iron in it! We have witnessed no game since the war in which fitter, better-conditioned, more determined men have taken part. It laughed at fear."*

It went on to say: *"The tackling was extraordinary; its effect was instantaneous; the man collared had to yield at once, but the New Zealanders won well. O'Brien was a great little man. He made no mistakes."*

The Daily Mail reported: *"A most strenuously fought game, contested in the best of spirits and was undoubtedly won by the better side: though New Zealand would be first to admit they had most of the luck."*

The Times felt: *"New Zealand has one of the finest sides ever seen in this country and O'Brien is a classic player,"* while the Athletic News concluded that: *"Victory in the end has gone to the cleverer, more adaptable and better side."*

While Belliss was noted for his fine scrummaging, Fea's handling of the ball was wonderful and he proved the perfect link.

The question now posed was: "How could the Mother Country halt the New Zealand machine in just seven days' time?"

The Times correspondent wrote: *"The Home Army team will have to be in its best form to win. The game will depend on the home forwards, who hitherto have not shown themselves to be a great pack. But it is never safe to venture a forecast of a match at Inverleith."* A close thing seemed to be on the cards.

New Zealand – *J G O'Brien; +W A Ford, *L B Stohr, +P W Storey; +W R Fea, *J Ryan (capt); *C Brown; A P Singe, *E W Hasell, R Sellars, E L J Cockcroft, *N A Wilson, J Kissick, +E A Belliss, +R Fogarty.

Tries – Storey, Ford, Hasell, Bellis. **Con** – Stohr.

South Africa – B F Windell; *W J Mills, T H Mills, D V Scully, +S W Harris; V St G Leger; +W H Townsend; *C A Riorden, +F W Mellish, A O Brownlee (capt), F A Bennetto, D Duncan, *+W H (Boy) Morkel (capt), D A St J Wolfe, J Schwartz.

Try – (WJ) Mills. **Con** – Scully.

Referee – Not known.

MATCH 11:
New Zealand v Mother Country
6-3

APRIL 5th 1919   **INVERLEITH**

No new players were introduced on either side to a match where New Zealand hung on like grim death in a tremendously tense game, which was easily the best of the tournament.

The sides were photographed together before the game, with the splendid Blackheath forward Peter Lawless proving the only player on the Mother Country side never to be capped.

Few more impressive sights in the history of rugby had been seen than when 'God Save the King' broke out before the start, well over 20,000 standing with soldiers saluting and civilians bare-headed in loyal tribute to the head of the empire and the donor of the trophy.

Hundreds of New Zealand soldiers had made the long trek to Scotland but the home supporters roared loudly as Australian-born Leo Brown led the Mother Country team out onto the pitch. All were to witness the greatest match of the season.

The Daily Telegraph noted: *"It began at a high rate and finished full of fury, with the Mother Country players almost incredibly strong and fighting to the last gasp; New Zealand, with their backs to the wall, refusing to yield and holding their lead with a grimness which won the warmest admiration from the spectators."*

In his 'Words of Passage: The Original', NZ journalist J Thomson

INTER-SERVICES RUGBY.

THE KING'S CUP.

The King, who is taking the greatest interest in the development of Army sport, will present a Challenge Cup to the winning team in the Inter-Services and Dominion Forces Competition.

The tournament, which, was begun on Saturday, March 1, extends over six weeks, finishing on Saturday, April 12. On the following Saturday the winners will be opposed by the French Army at Twickenham. Up to the present seven of the 15 matches in the competition have been decided, the record standing as follows:—Mother Country, two wins; New Zealand, two wins; South Africa, two wins, one loss; Australia, one win, one loss; Canada, two losses; R.A.F., three losses.

Three games will be played next Saturday. The Mother Country will meet Canada at Inverleith (Edinburgh), the R.A.F. and Australia will play at Gloucester, and New Zealand and South Africa will meet at Twickenham. The result of this last encounter must have an important bearing upon the result of the competition.

The remaining fixtures are :—

APRIL 5.
INVERLEITH.—Mother Country v. New Zealand.
TWICKENHAM.—Australia v. Canada.

APRIL 9.
BRADFORD.—New Zealand v. Australia.

APRIL 12
TWICKENHAM.—Mother Country v. South Africa.
LEICESTER —R.A.F. v. Canada.

Tension mounts in The Times

The teams: and there's that boy again! (Alexander Turnbull Library, New Zealand)

recorded it like this: *"By April it was clear that these two teams were rising to the top of the ladder..... the Inverleith ground was crammed, with thousands of our Diggers on leave and wearing the then-familiar lemon-squeezer hat."*

The Mother Country team played tremendously well and went extremely close to gaining the win, but New Zealand took their two first-half chances superbly. As usual it was their splendid wingers, Percy Storey and 'Jockey' Ford, who were at the heart of their attacks.

Their five-eighth and captain on the day, Jimmy Ryan was injured for a spell, while his opposite number, Wales' Clem Lewis, had a comparatively poor game. The Mother Country's best performers in the backs were full back Barry Cumberlege and centre Reg Pickles.

Programme Cover

Forward 'Cherry' Pillman took over the task of putting the 'home' ball into the scrum as the speedy NZ flanker Arthur Singe was on top of scrum half John Pym so quickly.

A tremendous maul on the line saw the powerful forward 'Moke' Bellis open the scoring for the All Blacks, before Storey took a hand with what Thomson, in his account, called *"...the best solo effort I have ever seen in first-class company.*

At a vital stage, Storey intercepted the ball in his own 25, shot off the mark like a bullet, veered slightly infield and side-stepped through a previously impregnable defensive line. With full back Cumberlege still to beat, we wondered what Storey would do, his

Inverleith Crowds (Alexander Turnbull Library, New Zealand)

Action from Inverleith (Alexander Turnbull Library, New Zealand)

terrific speed having left his support behind. Should he punt over the full back's head and risk the luck of the bounce?

No such thing. Not from the volatile Storey, He ran straight at Cumberlege, giving the impression that he might go right through him. Then, at the last second, he succeeded with still another lightning sidestep and was over the goal-line in a flash for a try.

The scene among the New Zealand groups around the ground can easily be imagined. Impromptu hakas broke out here and there, and Digger hats were thrown high in the air to become souvenirs for civilians..."

Some score! (Mind you, have you ever seen Obolensky's 'classic' second try in 1936 on film? Great directional switch, but was it overall quite as good as the memories of those there seemed to think?).

The Mother Country's pack, led by Pillman and Usher, had begun the game well, but Pillman had let a chance slip when he kicked instead of passed and Lewis missed with a drop shot, while Harold Day, from a pass by Cumberlege, was just held up short of the line.

New Zealand, who had won the toss, had temporarily lost Ryan in the first half with an ankle injury, but he soon returned, seemingly fit.

Some had thought that the Belliss try would have been ruled out with both packs on or over the line, but referee Cunningham awarded the score.

In the second half, the Mother Country pack battered at the New Zealand line and Pillman had a 'home' try disallowed for not grounding correctly, but when Lewis and Pickles handled, although William Cullen was tackled as he kicked ahead, winger Day defeated Ryan in a race for the ball to grab a Mother Country try.

It was now one-way traffic as the Mother Country turned up the heat, but New Zealand tackled and tackled. Cullen went for a drop-goal winner (then worth four points) only to see the ball go just wide.

O'Brien was safe and Singe outstanding and though Lewis took Pym's passes well, he was closely marked and not at his very best, while Pickles and Sloan were dangerous and Cumberlege a huge success at full back.

Sporting Life said: *"It was no disgrace to the Mother Country to lose, but had their forwards played in the first half as they did later, the visitors' defence would not have prevailed. The Colonial threequarters scarcely ever got going properly. The wing men never got a decent chance and the opening that Storey got, he had to make for himself."*

Athletic News commented: *"New Zealand were ever so slightly the better side. The irrepressible Storey is surely the discovery of the competition."*

It was a match played in a great spirit and New Zealand remained unbeaten, just needing to defeat Australia in four days' time to win the Cup outright.

It had been a fitting spectacle, living up to hopes and expectations, and leading one spectator to feel: "There is not much wrong with the British Empire when it can breed such men." That was the sentiment the establishment, at least at home, very much wanted to have engendered.

New Zealand – *J G O'Brien; +W A Ford, *L B Stohr, +P W Storey; G J McNaught, *J Ryan (capt); *C Brown; A P Singe, *E W Hasell, R Sellars, E L J Cockcroft, *N A Wilson, J Kissick, +E A Belliss, +R Fogarty.

Tries – Bellis, Storey.

Mother Country – +B S Cumberlege; +H L V Day, +W J Cullen, +R C W Pickles, *+A T Sloan; *+J C M Lewis, *J A Pym; *+C M Usher, *J S Brunton, *C H Pillman, *+L G Brown (capt), +C W Jones, *+A D Laing, P H Lawless, +R A Gallie.

Try – Day.

Referee – J G Cunningham (Watsonians).

MATCH 12:
Australia v Canada
38-0

APRIL 5th 1919   **TWICKENHAM**

Canada, perhaps worn down somewhat by a series of defeats at the hands of more experienced and increasingly well-drilled opposition, were able to offer little effective resistance before a crowd of around 4,000, as Australia scored four tries in the first half and six more in the second.

Canada wore numbers on their shirts but they were unnumbered on the programme, while Australia were numbered in the programme, but had none on the backs of their shirts. To confuse things even more, both sides wore blue jerseys, though of different shades!

The Prince of Wales and Prince Albert arrived just before the interval and the former had both sides presented to him after the game. Daniel Carroll, later capped by USA and who appeared in two Olympic Games victories, made an appearance at centre for Australia: just the sort of opposition reinforcement the Canadians could have done without!

The remarkable Daniel Carroll

The crowd willed Canada on but for the fourth successive game they failed to score, despite winger Pritchard going close.

Wing Dudley Suttor scored the first Australian try, followed by forwards Viv Dunn and John Bond. Before the interval the new Aussie fly half John Robertson went over, but 'Bluey' Thompson goaled only once for a 14-0 half-time lead.

Australia ran riot after the break as Robertson again, wing 'Pat' Egan and centre Daniel Carroll

Baines Australian shield

grabbed further tries, and as Canada tired Australia poured it on, with teenager 'Rat' Flanagan at scrum half calling the tune.

Forward Bill Bradley (twice) and the pacy Suttor, for his second, crossed, pack man Thompson kicking the final three conversions.

Canada's task in the competition was proving rather too much for them, but their courage would be remembered: now they hoped to make a fight of it against the RAF, in what would possibly be a last-ever rugby union match for many of their team.

Australia – *+B M Beith; *D C Suttor, *D B Carroll, H R Pountney, M (Pat) Egan; J Robertson, T W Flanagan; *W T Watson (capt), *+J H Bond, A M Lyons, +V A Dunn, *E A S Cody, W R Bradley, *J Thompson, G E See.

Tries – Robertson 2, Suttor 2, Bradley 2, Dunn, Bond, Egan, Carroll.
Cons – Thompson 4.

Canada – Pte Evans; J H Pritchard, C H Perry (capt), A M Grimmett, J D Phillips; G (or S J) Davies, D Davies; M A Hall, F A Herman, Sgt-Major Guthrie, Lieut Cochrane, R Wilson, T McQuarrie, Pte White, A M Nisbet.

Referee – Major Joseph Edward Crawshay ('Birdie') Partridge (Newport/South Africa).

MATCH 13:
New Zealand v Australia
5-6

APRIL 9ᵗʰ 1919   **LIDGET GREEN, BRADFORD**

This was the match postponed from March 22nd due to three inches of snow on the pitch, and results during the delay meant a New Zealand win would give them the cup. However, in the glorious way of sporting competition, it was to be a huge upset. New Zealand suffered a one-point defeat as Australia dug deep and handed the 'All Blacks' their first beating of the tournament.

Both sides had been in action just four days earlier, but it was thought by some to be a formality for New Zealand that would give them the Cup. Others believed that the great effort by the Mother Country had tired New

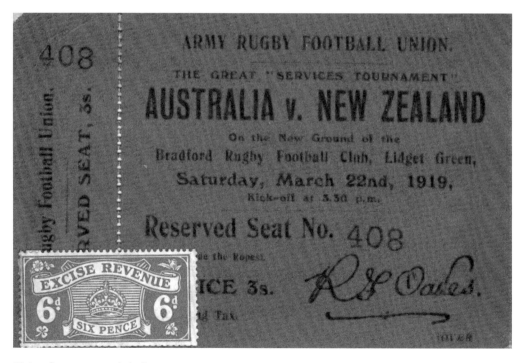

Ticket for postponed clash

Zealand – their pack in particular – and that Australia had the forwards to fully stretch them on the Lidget Green pitch.

Aussie skipper Bill Watson's policy was to move the ball to the open spaces in the first half and close the game up into the wind after the break, while also seeking to make sure that the dangerous match-winning New Zealand wingers, Percy Storey and 'Jockey' Ford, were starved of the ball. New Zealand aided their own downfall by passing the ball unusually slowly, and Australia may have won by more than one point had they not missed penalty chances at goal.

The result set the competition alight and meant that a Mother Country win over South Africa in three days' time would see both them and New Zealand achieve a record of four wins and one loss, triggering a play-off game at Twickenham.

It is interesting to note the comments of someone who well remembered the pre-schism days and the original 'colonial' tourists, and was also accustomed to seeing rugby played for a trophy. That Australian pack impressed one and all on the day, and at least prevented New Zealand from carrying off the King's Cup with games to spare. This newspaper cutting shows what 'Old Ebor' (the Welsh-born A W Pullin) made of the game in the local Yorkshire press.

In fine conditions a crowd of at least 6,000 saw Australia gain the advantage of winning the toss, electing to play with the wind and have the sun shining into New Zealand eyes. The Aussies led by 6-0 at the interval. 'Bluey' Thompson scored the first try when Jack O'Brien made a rare mistake and had his kick charged-down. Then, after full back Jackie Beith hit a post with a penalty some good Australian passing put in winger 'Pat' Egan for the second score, but neither was converted.

With the wind behind them, though with the sun receding, New Zealand clawed their way back into the game with an early second-half try by 'that man', Storey, which centre Jack Stohr converted.

There was just a point in it and New Zealand might have thought they could get the score they needed, but they had reckoned without the Australian forward effort, especially by their marauders in the loose. The tackling on both sides was hard, fair and solid yet the Australian pack won the day and finished the game the better.

So the Cup remained very much up for grabs, thanks in no small measure to Jimmy Clarken. Making his debut in the Cup, forwards coach Clarken was mainly responsible for disrupting the New Zealand 2-3-2 scrum formation: yet he was aged 42 years and 10 months at the time and the only new face on either side!

THE KING'S CUP.

SURPRISE MATCH AT BRADFORD.
(By OLD EBOR.)

It was like watching an old-time Bradford v. Wakefield Trinity cup-tie at Lidget Green yesterday evening. On the one side we had the All Blacks, with a back division that would need very few chances to put up a winning score; on the other there were the Australians who knew their strength forward and were determined to use it, and to make their opponents play a game foreign to their natural bent. The forwards prevailed, as they often do in such circumstances, and in especial when there is something in the nature of a challenge trophy to be fought for. There were old Bradford Rugby men on the Lidget Green ground yesterday—Rawson Robertshaw, Herbert Robertshaw, Laurie Hickson, "Jock" Potter, and "Jimmy" Wright—there may have been others; I saw Charlie Emmott, but he is of a later date—and I wondered if the play of the Australian forwards conjured up memories of cup-tie fights with Wakefield Trinity and Halifax!

The Australians really seemed to do their best to lose the match in the first half. That is to say they failed to take chances which players who are cool and assured of themselves make certain of. Two of the simplest shots at goal, straight in front of the posts, were missed; another dead straight and further up the field, but with the wind behind it, was not difficult. I should expect Ben Gronow to succeed with it nearly every time. On the other hand, the Australian backs were a bit unlucky in their attacks in this half. It is true their passing was too much of a lateral kind, but when tries are missed by inches, players may rightly think that fortune is against them. I know that when the only Australian scores in the first half were the tries by Thompson—a fine forward, this, of the Kewney type—and Egan, I considered, and so did the Colonials by me, that New Zealand had had the best of the luck, and that with the wind to aid them they had the match as good as won.

This opinion was strengthened by the ease with which Storey crowned a passing bout for New Zealand, and the success of Stohr in kicking a goal from near touch, after five minutes' play in the second half. Those who saw Storey score this try will understand what a difficult task Cumberlege was set at Edinburgh last Saturday, when he was Britain's last hope in an open field. It is not often a full back will bring a man of Storey's speed and swerving ability down in such circumstances. But after Storey's effort yesterday evening, so far from more tries and an easy victory following, the New Zealanders showed that they were being gradually but surely beaten. They were up against forwards who were as fresh as they were strong, and as determined as they were tactically skilful. It was only by desperate tackling, plus a little more bad luck on the attacking side, that the Australians were kept from scoring at least two more tries. Neither Thompson nor Suttor was more than a foot off the line when they were brought down. The "Blues"—they wore light blue jerseys—only won by a single point—6 to 5. It was sufficient, of course, but really the All Blacks were fortunate that the margin against them was not ten points instead of one.

The crowd, mustering I should say between six and eight thousand—a fine gate for an evening match—did not see the "spectacular" form of football in more than a few instances. Yet from the heartiness with which the Australian forwards were cheered, it was clear that they appreciated the grimness of their fight, as well as the clever tactical work of the forwards. There were Northern Union experts present, and though they may not have seen as much open passing and running as they would have liked to see, they did see methods of scrummaging, and of controlling the ball, and of heeling which one or two N.U. forward teams of my acquaintance might copy with advantage—if they are capable of doing so. The Australian forwards worked to system throughout. With the strong wind, they hooked and heeled generally; against it, and when it was above all things necessary to keep the New Zealand half-back and wing forward "guessing" they held the ball in the second row of the scrummage until the other fellows backs wearied and breath became shorter. Then they "went for them." They bustled and overran them. In the last quarter of an hour the All Blacks were a whipped side. Despite their wonderfully fine tackling they knew they were beaten.

The Yorkshire verdict of 'Old Ebor'

New Zealand –*J G O'Brien; +W A Ford, *L B Stohr, +P W Storey; *J Ryan (capt); D M Sandman, *C Brown; A P Singe, *E W Hasell, R Sellars, E L J Cockcroft, *N A Wilson, H G Whittington, +E A Belliss, A Gilchrist.

Try – Storey. **Con** – Stohr.

Australia – *+B M Beith; *D C Suttor, *D B Carroll, H R Pountney, M (Pat) Egan; J Robertson, T W Flanagan; *W T Watson (capt), +V A Dunn, *E A S Cody, W R Bradley, *J Thompson, G E See, J Murray, *J C Clarken.

Tries – Thompson, Egan.

Referee – Not known.

MATCH 14:
Royal Air Force v Canada
11-3

APRIL 12th 1919　　　　　**WELFORD RD, LEICESTER**

The match between two of the comparative strugglers went to form, but this was Canada's best effort and their pack generally held firm. It was scoreless at half-time and then Canada, playing with the wind behind them, led with not only their first try of the tournament, but also their only score.

It was obtained by their centre, Lieutenant Edward Watling, early in the second half. That try provoked the RAF side into action and when Taylor sparked an attack it ended with the equalising try by centre and skipper Godfrey Wrentmore: but generally Canada more than held their own up front, with the RAF's backs handling poorly.

Still, the airmen were now all out for the winner and Canada were forced back and back before the RAF struck twice more to gain the win. First their South African forward Hjalma Thesen put them ahead, then wing Tennant Sloan crossed to make the game safe.

The RAF's new centre Lieutenant Clarke converted with what proved the only successful goal of the whole match.

Canada's sole try scorer, Edward Watling

The Times said: *"It was a good match and Canada showed much better form than in any of their earlier games but their backs, although they defended pluckily, were lacking in initiative and the ability to attack."*

The same correspondent declared: *"For Canada the real value is a missionary one, for it is hoped that they will instill into Canadians the value of the game, which, despite climatic conditions, ought to be a real Canadian one."*

The RAF were running into some form as their combination settled and the games went on, and Wakefield comments: *"… we beat Canada at Leicester, and then completed the season by defeating Gloucester, Leicester and Neath on tour, though we just lost to Llanelly and Swansea.*

The tournament was a splendid opportunity during that transition period while men were waiting to be demobilised or be returned to their Dominions, to get Rugger started and also to see something of the best players from overseas… and it was almost the only organised Rugby football played in the spring of 1919, though a few clubs, such as Leicester, Gloucester and the big Welsh organisations, managed to collect sufficient of their old sides to play various Service and Dominion teams during March and April.

I mention the tournament because it was unique in rugby history for footballers representing so many parts of the Empire to play against one another, and … in this series of games Northern Union players were made eligible by a special dispensation.

Billy Seddon taught me the secret of spin-kicking. He was a very fine kick himself, and won more than one match for us with his long-range dropped goals. H W Taylor, the South African cricket captain, was also a member of our team, and a most useful centre or stand-off: his taking of passes being especially good. We had several other South Africans, such as J P Finlay, who afterwards did well in SA football, and G M Wrentmore, who had been with me at Cranwell and captained our Inter-Service League side, while I led the forwards, taking over the captaincy when he was unable to play.

We had with us George Thom, and I remember during the 1920 Scotland match, when I jumped for the ball in the line-out he dug his fingers into my ribs, knowing me to be ticklish, and secured the ball while I was doubled up. When I straightened myself, there was Thom looking at me and roaring with laughter! We had two other Scotland internationals, A W Symington, who also played for Cambridge, and R S Simpson, who captained Glasgow Academicals after the war. Simpson showed me the value of going down on a ball and stopping rushes before they got going, an art at which he was particularly adept."

RAF – W Seddon (RL); J L Hamilton, W G Clarke, G M Wrentmore (capt), *L H T Sloan; *F M Taylor, L Rendles; +W W Wakefield, +G Thom, +R S Simpson, A H Malan, E F Turner, J P Findlay, H H Thesen, C W Thompson.

Tries – Wrentmore, Thesen, Sloan. **Con** – Clarke.

Canada – J Holland; J H Pritchard, E W W Watling, A M Grimmett, J D Phillips; G Edwards (capt), D Davies; Sergeant-Major Guthrie, R Wilson, T McQuarrie, A M Nisbet, Sergeant Light, Sergeant Houson, Sergeant Herman, H J McDonald.

Try – Watling.

Referee – Not known.

MATCH 15:
Mother Country v S Africa
21-12

APRIL 12th 1919   **TWICKENHAM**

This was the 15th and potentially the final match of the tournament, as failure to win by the Mother Country would mean that New Zealand would be crowned winners. However, that was not to be.

The Mother Country's win at Twickenham forced a play-off with New Zealand, as when the final whistle blew, both had lost just once. There were 12,000 present to see the South African pack outplay the home side, but find themselves beaten behind the scrum.

Though his side were without wing Harold Day, who had fallen out with injury, Welsh fly half Clem Lewis was at his best for the Mother Country. In Day's place for this crucial clash Major E G W W Harrison (Royal Field Artillery) had been selected, but he too withdrew.

James Dickson of Ireland was called in, while another Irishman, international Herbert Moore, replaced the injured 'Podger' Laing in the pack. The *History of Army Rugby* stated that Harrison played, but that was incorrect.

Dickson had the huge role of marking the brilliant wing Stan Harris and he was beaten just the once, but it was Lewis who was the match-winner. He started by pouncing on an error by the new full back, de Villiers, with the Welshman almost sending Allen Sloan over.

Then, seconds later, the combination produced a try for Sloan, though Cumberlege missed the conversion, and soon after, it was Lewis again who made a break and sent William Cullen in for a try with skipper Leo G 'Bruno' Brown converting.

The Cardiff and Wales fly half was at it again after another de Villiers fumble, and he kicked on with Scotland forward Charles Usher being first to the ball over the line and Brown again landing the extras.

Next came a try for centre Reg Pickles after Usher hacked on and Wally Mills made a hash of it, allowing the Bristol player to touch down. Brown missed the conversion and although it was 16-0 it was far from over.

Herbert Moore

As the rain poured down, centre Scully missed with a dropped goal attempt just minutes before scoring with another. It was 16-4 at the interval, during which, Princes Albert and Henry arrived at the ground.

The South African forwards upped their game and when the Mother Country did heel, 'Taffy' Townsend was quick to catch Pym, but skipper Brown recovered and burst away, scored and converted and it was 21-4. However, South Africa hit back again with splendid passing that finished with Harris tearing in at the corner, de Villiers just failing to convert.

Once more South Africa came forward and scrum half Townsend backed up his pack to score, with Scully converting. The Mother Country were being forced back but Lewis, with splendid kicking and a fine run, helped relieve the pressure.

Then Harris burst through again, but Dickson was equal to it and stopped him: for the 'Springboks' it was too little, too late.

The Mother Country had done what they needed too, and that winner-takes-all play-off match was beckoning, with Twickenham once again the venue.

Mother Country – +B S Cumberlege; +J A N Dickson, +W J Cullen, +R C W Pickles, *+A T Sloan; *+J C M Lewis, *J A Pym; *+C M Usher, *J S Brunton, *C H Pillman, *+L G Brown (capt), +C W Jones, P H Lawless, *H B Moore, +R A Gallie.

Tries – Sloan, Cullen, Usher, Pickles, Brown. **Cons** – Brown 3.

South Africa – I B de Villiers; *W J Mills, T H Mills, D V Scully, +S W Harris; R F Windell; +W H Townsend; *+W H Morkel (capt), *W A Burger, *C A Riorden, +F W Mellish, M Versfield, F A Bennetto, D Duncan, D A St J Wolfe.

Tries – Harris, Townsend. **Con** – Scully. **DG** – Scully.

Referee – Not known.

THE PLAY-OFF MATCH:
New Zealand v Mother Country
9-3

APRIL 16th 1919   **TWICKENHAM**

Could the Mother Country reverse the Inverleith result and claim the Cup to which George V had given his name? Or would the men from 12,000 miles away who had come to fight for that King and all 'his' countries maintain their edge and build on the winning reputation they and their countrymen had built over the previous 15 years?

It seems rather fitting, if unusual, that there should have been a play-off planned, for in an era before such competitions (remember how hard it was for the RFU to agree to, and actually call it, a 'Cup' competition in the 1970s?), a rather anti-climactic 'tie' or countback of points would have perhaps seemed more likely.

Indeed, this newspaper report pictured here, from one of the earlier games, suggests that just such an alternative ending had been intended. Was it meant to be decided on points difference, with the result that the Mother Country would have won? At all events, it was well-known in plenty of time that a play-off was eventually planned, and that meant a very exciting finale to a competition that appears to have moved along with close-to-military precision.

The honour of representing the British Empire against France, and of winning the King's Cup, now depends upon the match between Great Britain and South Africa at Twickenham next Saturday. Should the Mother Country's team win, they and the New Zealanders will be equal in points, 8 each out of a possible 10. But this emergency has been provided against. The championship will, in that event, be decided by the score points, and these are already in the Mother Country's favour, alike in attack and defence. It may be remembered that the New Zealanders played a reserve team against Canada on the day they met Yorkshire. By so doing they surrendered a probable harvest of points. I wonder if the "All Blacks" will now lose the King's Cup through loyalty in fulfilling their engagement with Yorkshire with a representative team?

The table (overleaf) makes the point that the Mother Country had the best record overall, but in all fairness the All Blacks had prevailed in the head-to head-game. Now they had the chance to repeat that feat in a final showdown and showcase at the new headquarters of rugby: and repeat it they did.

New Zealand won the play-off, and thus the King's Cup, in front of some 10,000 spectators who included the Prince of Wales and the Rt Hon. William F ('Bill')

Massey, the Prime Minister of New Zealand, as well as many British and Dominion servicemen.

Mother Country	won 4 lost 1	(81-27)	8 pts
New Zealand	won 4 lost 1	(58-17)	8 pts
Australia	won 3 lost 2	(58-23)	6 pts
South Africa	won 2 lost 3	(65-43)	4 pts
RAF	won 2 lost 3	(27-69)	4 pts
Canada	won 0 lost 5	(3-113)	0 pts

Noticeably, but typically of the time, while the New Zealand side contained one officer and 14 others, the Mother Country fielded 14 officers plus CSM Jones. They made one late change as Wales international, Reverend Bill Havard, replaced the injured Joseph Brunton in the pack and for New Zealand, Jim Moffitt and Alf West made their debuts in the tournament. Both won their full international caps later with West, who became a full All Black in 1921, returning to GB in 1924 with Cliff Porter's 'Invincible' tourists.

Every New Zealander appeared at tip-top fitness, with their pack outstanding. Wingers Percy Storey and 'Jockey' Ford were the stars, with Ford looking the complete player and the 'find' of the year. Strangely, however, he was never to win a full international cap.

CSM Charles Jones

New Zealand had most of the early ball, but both William Cullen and Allen Sloan had good runs in reply, then full back Barry Cumberlege kicked the Mother Country ahead with a penalty on 20 minutes. Before the interval, though, New Zealand, playing with the wind, levelled when centre Jack Stohr landed a penalty.

'Peter' Lawless of the Mother Country later wrote: "*Playing against New Zealand at Twickenham in 1919, we went off against a terrific wind, blowing over the mound where the North Stand was later to raise its gaunt covering. We did well enough in the*

Joseph Brunton: out of the game but later, RFU President

first half, and crossed over full of confidence, only a try to the bad. But we little knew how much energy we had expended against that hurricane, and in the end were soundly beaten".

In the second half, New Zealand came on and on, denying the Mother Country any ball, then Ford tore down the left wing outpacing the defence for a try. Although Stohr could not convert, it gave his side a lead they were not to lose.

It was pressure that led to the final score as loose forward Arthur Singe, a truly magnificent spoiler, went over from a close-range scrum. 'Moke' Belliss, 'Ranji' Wilson and Singe were the pick of a splendid New Zealand pack, making some of the home side look as if age (and the wind) had caught up with them.

Our New Zealand chronicler, Mr Thomson, commented: *"My old Otago Boys' High School fellow pupil, Billy Fea, was back after injury and distinguished himself by dictating the course of back play in our favour",* while writing 20 years on, another New Zealander, W F Ingram, recalled how a friend present at Twickenham for the play-off, had recounted a story about their war-time Premier. Mr Massey was a genuine rugby fan and very keen for his country to walk tall.

It appears that "Old Bill," as he was affectionately termed, *"...went into the New Zealand dressing-room at half-time, and wore a worried look. Things had not gone too good for the New Zealanders, and Mr. Massey approached one of the husky forwards and urged him to 'do his best for New Zealand; the people back home look forward to success.' There came an unexpected reply: 'Leave 'em to us, Bill! Politics might be your game, but this is our picnic!'*

In the second spell the New Zealanders used steam-roller tactics and gave the clever English backs no chances. After the final whistle Mr. Massey once again visited the dressing-room, but this time he wore a triumphant smile. His friend, the husky forward, was taking a shower. Mr. Massey grasped his hand, shook it with great fervour and stood there completely oblivious of the fact that the shower was on and that he was being drenched!"

The Auckland Star commented: *"The New Zealand forwards were as fresh as paint, but the Mother Country forwards were much the worse for wear and tear."*

William Cullen, capped the following year by Ireland, stood out as the best home player. Fly half Clem Lewis, though, did not look well and after the match he was admitted to Queen Mary's Military Hospital in Millbank with a high temperature and inflammation of the shin bone.

By then, though, New Zealand had the victory, and were to raise both the King's Cup and, still further, their reputation in the rugby-playing world. The Services tourney had been a major success and provided an outstanding sequence of games, which had helped put rugby back on the big stage.

The teams in that series-deciding game for 'the First World Cup' were:

New Zealand – *J G O'Brien; +W A Ford, *L B Stohr, +P W Storey; *J Ryan (capt), +W R Fea; *C Brown; A P Singe, *E W Hasell, *N A Wilson, +E A Belliss, J Kissick, *M J Cain, +J E Moffitt, +A H West.

Tries – Ford, Singe. **Pen** – Stohr.

Mother Country – +B S Cumberlege; +J A N Dickson, +W J Cullen, +R C W Pickles, *+A T Sloan; *+J C M Lewis, *J A Pym; *+C M Usher, +Rev W T Havard, *C H Pillman, *+L G Brown (capt), +C W Jones, P H Lawless, *H B Moore, +R A Gallie.

Pen – Cumberlege.

Referee – Mr Carver (England).

New Zealand with the King's Cup (Alexander Turnbull Library, New Zealand)

THE CHALLENGE MATCH: New Zealand v France 20-3

APRIL 19th 1919   TWICKENHAM

The King's Cup winners met a France side for a challenge match just three days after defeating the Mother Country. It was a great success, played in perfect weather, and a crowd of some 15,000 – the vast majority being soldiers – saw King George V present the King's Cup to Jimmy Ryan before the game.

The King's four sons (Albert, Henry, George and Edward, Prince of Wales), Field-Marshal Sir Douglas Haig, Sir Henry Wilson, the French Embassy staff and the New Zealand High Commissioner were all present.

New Zealand made two changes in their pack as Leslie Cockcroft and Dick Fogarty came in for 'Moke' Belliss and 'Ranji' Wilson. France apparently made several changes to their original selection, with scrum half Lieutenant Domercq being replaced by Dussert, Rene Crabos coming in at centre for Sergeant Lasserre and up front Eugene Soulie for Private Desdouge.

(It is assumed the absent Lasserre was Rene ('Poulet') Lasserre, 23, 15 caps (as forward and back) from 1914-1924. He also played in the 1924 Olympics. He was a pilot/sergeant in the French Flying Corps, and died in 1965.)

Referee Partridge made mistakes galore – perhaps, with his nickname, deserving 'the bird' from the crowd, but France, the chief sufferers, seemingly accepted every decision with impeccable grace.

The New Zealand forwards scored four of the six tries and both wing 'Jockey' Ford and loose forward Arthur Singe were again outstanding, as was the French full back Mazarico, whose kicking always found touch and who tackled fearlessly as well as diving at the feet of numerous New Zealand foot rushes.

Souvenir Programme

The King presents the Cup to Jimmy Ryan (Alexander Turnbull Library, New Zealand)

The Teams at 'Twickers' (Alexander Turnbull Library, New Zealand)

Action from the Challenge Match (Alexander Turnbull Library, New Zealand)

France opened the scoring when skipper and fly half Philippe Struxiano sent to Crabos, who dummied and put fellow-centre Rieu over. Stohr missed a penalty and Ford hit the crossbar with a drop shot before Singe touched down for 3-3 at the interval. France was going well and very much still in the match.

After the interval, though, New Zealand took charge, with 'Nut' Hasell and Alf West crossing, but Hasell failed with the conversions and when he

'Entente Cordiale': in rugby (Alexander Turnbull Library, New Zealand)

L'ENTENTE CORDIALE
Une partie de Football

...and in the recent conflict

was awarded a penalty in front of the posts he was applauded for deliberately missing, as the decision by referee Partridge appeared totally unjust.

The All Black pack had now got on top and Jack Kissick became the fourth forward to score as the French defence began to tire, though Ryan missed the conversion. Scrum half Charles Brown, who was to be elected captain by the players for the subsequent tour to South Africa, then touched down after strong forward play and Ford added the sixth and final try with Ryan kicking the only conversion of the afternoon.

The Times stated: *"Although the football did not reach a high level, the match was a great success. The game was fast; good play on either side was hailed with generous applause. It was more than a mere football match, it had more the character of a national festival. There was more than the usual warmth in the cheers which greeted the French team. It was as if the crowd was trying to voice its sympathy with our Allies for their sufferings in the past and its pleasure in sharing with them the joy of success: it was a true 'Victory' match."*

New Zealand – *J G O'Brien; +W A Ford, *L B Stohr, +P W Storey; *J Ryan (capt), +W R Fea; *C Brown; A P Singe, E L J Cockroft, R Fogarty, J Kissick, *M J Cain, +J E Moffitt, +A H West, *E W Hasell.

Tries – Singe, Hasell, West, Kissick, Brown, Ford. **Con** – Ryan.

France – Sergeant Mazarico; +J Etcheberry, +R Crabos, Lieutenant Rieu, Major/Adjutant (Doctor) Loubatie; *+P Struxiano (capt), Sub-Lieutenant Dussert; Major Dilleseger, +A Cassayet, +R Thierry, Sub-Lieutenant Galliax, Sub-Lieutenant Nicolai, +F Vaquer, +P Pons, +E Soulie.

Try – Rieu.

Referee – Major J E C ('Birdie') Partridge (Newport/South Africa).

Nine of this French side later played in a 45-6 win over Romania at Stade Colombes, Paris in June. It was a match as part of the Inter-Allied Games organized there to celebrate the end of the War. The United States also entered a team and though they too were too strong for Romania by 23-0, they lost 8-3 to France.

France, who had played a full part in a great day, were staying at the Imperial Hotel in Russell Square and after the game both teams dined there, in Oddeninho's Restaurant. That dinner was presided over by Major-General Sir C H Harington, KCB, DSO, whose speech took very much a rugby view of the war. After stating that His Majesty wished to give medals to both

France beat Romania, 1919

sides, he stretched the rugby team metaphor to (and beyond?) its limits in carrying on:

…..*"The War has been won by the Allies playing the game and playing it well and playing for the side. Decisive results were obtained when the whole team played together under the captaincy of that great soldier, Marshal Foch, who developed his attacks splendidly by means of those loyal and unselfish three-quarter backs – Sir Douglas Haig, General Pershing and the King of the Belgians and those good, outstanding forwards – our respective Army commanders.*

"Nor must we forget those wing three-quarters in distant theatres – namely our Commanders in Egypt, Macedonia, Mesopotamia, Italy and Russia – where our forces all helped so much to increase the score.

"Behind all that we had that sound full-back, represented by the men and women of all Allied nations….."

After the dinner, the speeches and the plaudits, though, there was precious little relaxation for the New Zealanders: just two days later, they were facing Wales in an international at Swansea!

6

The King's Cup Winners are Challenged by Wales

'Why go home? This was a rugby tour!'

Wales, doubtless keen for a crowd, another crack at the 'All Blacks' at 'official' level 14 years on, and a chance to show what they could do as a nation outside the 'umbrella' of the Mother Country side, awarded full international caps for this match: their first 'capped' Test in five years.

New Zealand did not, noting the essentially Services nature of this side, however strong, and which in one combination or another had already played 39 times in Britain.

Wales v NZ Services, April 1919

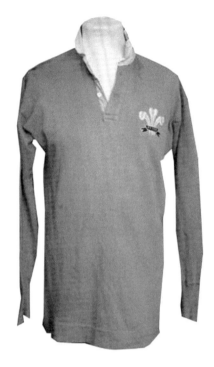

Gwyn Francis' Welsh Jersey

Scorer Jerry Shea

Six of the New Zealand team were already internationals and six were to be capped later. Jack Kissick and the brilliant loose forward Arthur Singe remained uncapped, while full back Capper played later for Western Samoa. All 15 had taken part in the King's Cup tournament and only Capper and Dick Fogarty had not played in the final.

They'd all worn the All Black jersey, though, even if the various tour pictures show that not all the players always had a Silver Fern on their jerseys: was that maybe just the shortage of 'non-essentials' in those hard times and with a plethora of rugged games?

Shea was another of the multi-talented performers of that era. He was to make history by becoming the first player at international level to achieve the 'full house' of a try, conversion, drop goal, and penalty goal (then 16 points) when Wales beat England 19-5 in 1920. In December 1921 he turned professional, joining Wigan for a then record fee of £700, and becoming a dual code international soon after. Shea was also a professional boxer at welter and middleweight, giving the Scottish RU another chance to berate the WRU for picking the 'Pill Pugilist'. Shea never fought for a major belt, but faced several notables during his nine-year career. He drew with and beat British and Commonwealth champion Frank Moody, then lost to former World Welterweight champion Ted 'Kid' Lewis at Mountain Ash. In 1921 he lost an eliminator for another crack at Lewis, but had, in 1920, beaten future European champion Rene DeVos, and in 1922 was to defeat future British light-heavyweight champion Gipsy Daniels. His final recorded fight was in November 1924 when he outpointed the ex-welterweight champion, Johnny Basham.

New Zealand had of course defeated the Mother Country in the King's Cup five days earlier, and France just two days previously. Wales had also been in action 48 hours before, and had drawn

Action at Swansea (Alexander Turnbull Library, New Zealand)

20,000 plus crowd (Alexander Turnbull Library, New Zealand)

3-3 (with a try by forward Aaron Rees) against the 38th Welsh Division at Swansea, the same venue as for the international.

Do we hear the odd moans from the RWC teams of today about short turnarounds in hectic tournament competition? This was easier than a war, anyway....

An Easter Monday afternoon crowd of some twenty-odd thousand was not, however, rewarded with a try. The game was not of the highest standard, with New Zealand better at forward but both sides defending well. Full back Evan Davies and scrum half Ike Fowler were the best Welsh players on the day.

As ever, Singe stood out as the best forward on the field but it was Wales who led from a Shea penalty after eight minutes, when Alf West (who was to be the only player from the NZ ranks to return to Britain with the 1924 All Blacks) was caught offside.

However, Jack Stohr placed two penalties before the interval – the second, from half-way, would have been retaken if missed as the Welsh forwards had charged and 'no charge' had been ruled by the English referee.

Martin had a spell off the field after taking a cut on the head, which led to the New Zealanders' studs being examined. Whether with 14 or 15, though, Wales could not get a score, and the tradition of very tight, low-scoring clashes between these two rugby-besotted nations continued. Once again, however, despite the hectic schedule, New Zealand had shown that vital winning edge.

With the ladies... (Alexander Turnbull Library, New Zealand)

April 21, 1919 – Wales 3 New Zealand Army XV 6
St. Helen's, Swansea - Attendance 20,000+

WALES – +E Davies; +J Shea, +B M G Thomas, +E B Rees, +T J Nicholas; *+W J Martin, +I J Fowler; *+G Stephens (capt), +J Jones, +Rev W T Havard, +D G Francis, +J J Whitfield, +A Rees, +W G H Morris, +E T Parker.

Pen – Shea.

NEW ZEALAND SERVICES – +C H Capper; +W A Ford, *L B Stohr, +P W Storey; *J Ryan (capt), +W R Fea: *C Brown; A P Singe, *E W Hasell, *M J Cain, +J E Moffitt, *N A Wilson, J Kissick, +A H West, +R Fogarty.

Pens – Stohr 2.

Referee – Robert R Charman (S Shields/Durham). Born S Shields 1883.

For Wales: Full back EVAN ('Ianto') DAVIES and forwards James (JIM) JONES and Edwin Thomas (TOM) PARKER are all detailed in the 1918 Wales XV match, when Davies played at centre. Another forward, the Reverend William Thomas (BILL) HAVARD is detailed in the King's Cup Teams section, when playing for the Mother Country.

The other 12 players were:

Jeremiah (Jerry) SHEA – Wing (later centre). Born Newport 12/8/1892. Died Caerleon 30/6/1947. Pill Harriers/Newport (63 games), 4 caps (1919-21). Rugby League for Wigan (85 games, 27 tries). Also a professional welter/middleweight boxer and professional runner.

Beriah Melbourne Gwynne THOMAS – Centre (later wing). Born Nantymoel 11/6/1896. Died Pontypridd 23/6/1966. Bridgend County School/University College, Cardiff/St Bartholomew's Hospital/London University/Ogmore Vale/Bridgend/London Welsh/Cardiff/Barbarians. 6 caps (1919-24). Doctor and surgeon, Sub-Lieutenant in the Navy.

Evan B REES – Centre. Born Cwmavon 9/8/1896. Died in the last quarter of 1978 in the Bridgend area. This was his only cap. Morriston/Aberavon/Swansea/Llanelli (one game). Rugby League for

Dewsbury/Wales (2 caps). Clerical Assistant for a textile company. Played for both Swansea and Llanelli against Maoris, 1919. Served in South Wales Borderers in WW1.

Trevor John NICHOLAS – Wing. Born Sudbrook 7/1/1894. Died Minehead 13/3/1979. Cardiff/Ebbw Vale/ Penarth. This was his only cap and came after only three games with Cardiff, for whom he played 39 times with 24 tries from 1919-20 until 1925-26. He served in the 38th Welsh Division and became a clerk in the National Coal Board.

Trevor Nicholas' Welsh Jersey

Walter John MARTIN, DCM – Outside Half. Born Woodford, Essex 15/5/1883. Died Newport 30/4/1933. Evesham School/Newport High School/University College, Cardiff/Newport/ Monmouthshire. 3 caps (1912-19). Company Sergeant-Major in the South Wales Borderers. Decorated for gallantry, carrying a wounded man under heavy shell fire. Worked for an accountancy firm and also was a railway official in Newport Docks. Sadly, committed suicide by hanging aged 49, when he was suffering terminal cancer. The game between the Barbarians and a Newport and District XV in 1933 was his memorial match.

Isaac John (Ike) FOWLER – Scrum half. Born Pantyffynnon 27/8/1894. Died Batley 17/6/1981. Tycroes/Pantycelyn/Ammanford/Llanelli. Played Rugby League for Batley and Wales. This was his only cap and because he 'went north' he did not receive it from the Welsh Rugby Union until 1975. In mining, then a foreman in a Batley textile factory.

Glyn Hopkin STEPHENS – Forward. Born Neath 29/11/1891. Died Neath 22/4/1965. Cadoxton Church School/ Wales Schools under-15/ Neath. 10 caps (1912-19). Mining engineer & owner/company director/ chairman of Port Talbot Magistrates. Welsh Rugby Union President in

1956-57. His son, Rees, won 32 caps (1947-57) and was a British Lion in New Zealand/Australia (2 tests) in 1950. They were the first and so far, only, father and son to captain Wales.

David Gwynn (Gwyn) FRANCIS – Forward. Born Gorseinon 2/2/1896. Died Reading 7/5/1987. Gowerton Grammar School/Aberystwyth Univ/ University College, Cardiff/Jesus College, Oxford University (Blue 1919)/Gorseinon/Loughor/Llanelli/L Welsh/Leicester/London Counties/ Surrey. 2 caps (1919-24). Became a referee and Berkshire RU President. Staff-Sergeant in the Royal Welch Fusiliers. Headmaster at Reading School. Sergeant-Instructor at Heston Command School of Musketry at Altcar and then Lieutenant in the 38th Welsh Division.

John James (Jack) WHITFIELD – Forward. Born Newport 23/3/1892. Died Newport 26/12/1927. Pill Harriers/ Newport (170 games, 42 tries). 12 caps (1919-24). Fitter in Newport Docks, then pub licensee in Newport. Died in the Royal Gwent Hospital after an operation for a gastric ulcer.

Aaron REES – Forward. Born Maesteg c 1886. Died Swansea 22/1/1950. Kenfig Hill/Maesteg. This was his only cap. He was a collier/hewer. Skippered Maesteg 1912 to 1914 and 1919-1920. He spent 1925-1931 living in Canada. Died in Swansea Hospital.

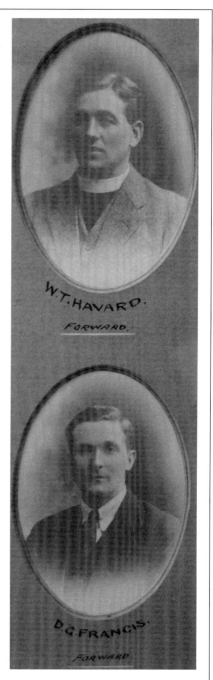

Havard & Francis: together for College and Country

William George Henry (Bill) MORRIS – Forward. Born Abertillery c.1894. Died Bournemouth 14/7/1967. Blaenau Gwent/Pill Harriers/ Abertillery/London Welsh. 3 caps (1919-21). Collier (his father owned a colliery), then an Education Welfare Officer. Skippered Abertillery 1919-1920 and from 1925 until 1928.

7

Home to New Zealand via Segregated South Africa

'Introducing politics into sport'

At the end of the King's Cup, the South African Rugby Board invited the New Zealand Army team to play 12 matches on the way home (it later turned out to be 15). Two years before the first ever All Black-Springbok Tests, this was a crucial and defining moment in the relationship between those who became the game's historically hegemonic powers: for at the prior request of the SARB, acceded to by the New Zealanders, the great forward 'Ranji' Wilson and five-eighth Parakura Tureia were not considered for selection, because they were 'coloured' players. The die of allowing the South African hosts to dictate the content of tourists' teams had been cast.

It appears that though the South African High Commissioner in London, W P Schreiner, who extended the invitation, was satisfied with coloured players being in the team, his son, Bill Schreiner, voted against at the decisive SARB meeting. Wilson, one of those barred, has been described by trusted judges as '...a flanker with true devilry, who in the years up to 1914 was acknowledged as the best loose-forward in New Zealand, which then, as now, meant very likely the best in the world.' As a ten times capped All Black he was a natural choice for their King's Cup side, and though 'Sergeant Wilson' was now 33, he was in no way a candidate for 'Dad's Army': rather, he was an obvious choice for the 'real' NZ Army's touring squad.

Instead, NZ, for their part, appeared to accept the situation and Wilson actually helped select the side, which, though Jimmy Ryan was still available and was vice-captain, was now skippered by Charles Brown, who had won the captaincy after a poll of all the players.

As Huw Richards writes: 'So, from 1919 until 1970 New Zealand were to allow South Africa to dictate the composition of its touring teams there. In the context of 'introducing politics into sport', it should be remembered that it was the South Africans who started it – a long time before 1948s introduction of formal apartheid.

It was also a fundamental breach of rugby's defining team epic - that an offence to a team-mate is an offence to all...... the context of a team drawn from men who for four years had been fighting and dying together makes it all the more shocking. Wilson evidently took this betrayal with dignity. Terry McLean records that he 'did not seem too disappointed'. At home he played 13 times for Wellington, including 11 defences of the Ranfurly Shield, and was on the selection panel for the 1924-5 'Invincible' All Black tourists.

If that remains one of the finest hours in NZ's unmatched rugby history, what happened five years earlier may be its shabbiest. Challenged to stand by the most basic of rugby's supposed values, it flunked the test. Wilson may have been the immediate loser, but the stain on the game in general – and New Zealand in particular – extended much further and longer.'

NZ Services Team touring S Africa, 1919

The tour was managed by Lieut. R Walter (Wally) Baumgart of Wellington and the Otago Rifle Brigade, with Lieut. E W King of Wellington as assistant manager. King, in fact, made some tour appearances on the wing. P W Day of the South African Rugby Board also accompanied the tour party.

On June 21 the New Zealand party – with all their players given higher ranks in the Army prior to leaving – left Plymouth on board the Cap Paloma en route to Cape Town.

One player had joined the team:

> **John Alexander (Alex) BRUCE** – Forward. Born Wellington 11/11/1887. Died Wellington 20/10/1970. To Aro School/St James RFC/Wellington/ Athletic RFC/Auckland/City RFC/North Island. 2 caps (1914). A carpenter, he had toured with New Zealand to America in 1913 and to Australia in 1914. A Sapper, later a Sergeant in the Field Engineers, based at Boscombe Camp. (Some say he played in the King's Cup, but there is no record of it).

Not unusually for the time, there is some dispute over the detailed statistics of the tour: but it appears that eleven of the games were won, three lost and one drawn, with a points tally of 170-68. P W Storey played in the first 14 matches, missing only the final one, and supposedly scoring seven tries, though other sources suggest it may be eight or nine!

The 15 matches were as follows:

> **July 24, 1919 – Western Province Country Club 6 NZ Army 8**
> **Newlands, Cape Town – Attendance 12,000**
>
> **WPCC** – Try – M Versfield. Pen – Metcalfe. (Versfield had played in the King's Cup).
>
> **NZ** – Tries – J A Bruce, R W Roberts. Con – L B Stohr.
>
> The South African Premier, General Botha, had arrived back in Cape Town from England that day and greeted the team.

> **July 26, 1919 – Western Province Town Clubs 3 NZ Army 3**
> **Newlands, Cape Town – Attendance 20,000**
>
> **WPTC** – Try – Botha.
>
> **NZ** – Try – P W Storey.

> **July 29, 1919 – South-West Province 0 NZ Army 23**
> **Oudtshoorn – Attendance 3,000**
>
> **NZ** – Tries – W A Ford 2, J E Moffitt 2, P W Storey, A H West, J Ryan. Con – E W Hasell.

153

August 2, 1919 – Eastern Province 0 NZ Army 15
Crusaders Ground, Port Elizabeth – Attendance 8,000

NZ – Tries – A P Singe, D M Sandman, E A Belliss, W A Ford. Pen – J Ryan.

Eastern Province were captained by Thomas Frederick van Vuuren, an international forward with five caps, all won when he toured with the Springboks to GB/France in 1912-13.

August 6, 1919 – Orange Free State 5 NZ Army 16
Ramblers Ground, Bloemfontein

OFS – Try – Serfontein. Con – Mentz.

NZ – Tries – W A Ford, A H West, P W Storey, A E Belliss. Cons – E W Hasell, A H West.

The leading home player was Evelyn Edgar ('Boetie') McHardy, a wing with five caps all gained on the Springboks 1912-13 tour of GB/France.

August 9, 1919 – Griqualand West 8 NZ Army 3
Kimberely

GW – Tries – Corporal F A Bennetto, F J Dobbin. Con – S S F Strauss.

NZ – Pen – E W Hasell.

Dobbin was Frederick James ('Uncle') Dobbin, then 40, who won nine caps (1903-12). Strauss was Saril Stephanus Francois Strauss, who won a cap for South Africa (1921). Bennetto had played in the King's Cup. While at Kimberley, the Griqualand West Rugby Union presented each New Zealand player with a gold medallion inset with an uncut diamond from the Kimberley mines. For NZ both Henry and Moffitt retired with injury.

August 13, 1919 – Witwatersrand 0 NZ Army 6
Wanderers Ground, Johannesburg – Attendance 15,000

NZ – Try – P W Storey. Pen – L B Stohr.

Witwatersrand included internationals in:

Douglas Francis Theodore Morkel (nine caps, 1906-13);
John Douglas Luyt (seven caps, 1910-13);
Joseph Adrian Jooste Francis (five caps, 1912-13);
A de la R van der Hoff (uncapped),

all of whom had toured with the Springboks to GB/France in 1912-13;

and George W ('Tank') van Rooyen (two caps, 1921), who toured New Zealand in 1921 and later switched to rugby league with Hull/Wigan/Widnes.

August 16, 1919 – Rand Mines 3 NA Army 24
Wanderers Ground, Johannesburg

RM – Try – J A J Francis.

NZ – Tries – A E Belliss 2, J A Bruce, W A Ford. Cons – L B Stohr 3. Pens – Stohr 2.

Francis, Douglas Morkel and van Rooyen had also played for Witwatersrand, while the Rand Mines side also included Ernest Hamilton ('Baby') Shum, who won a cap on the 1912-13 Springboks tour to GB/France.

August 20, 1919 – Pretoria 4 NZ Army 5
Pretoria

P – DG – von Quitzlow.

NZ – Try – C Brown. Con – L B Stohr.

Skipper Charlie Brown got the vital converted try, which was at that time worth one more than the four points then secured by a dropped goal.

August 23, 1919 – Transvaal 3 NZ Army 5
Wanderers Ground, Johannesburg – Attendance 22,000

T – Pen – Clark.

NZ – Try – E A Belliss. Con – L B Stohr.

Transvaal included Clifford Atherton Riorden, who played in the King's Cup and had won two caps in 1910. Belliss received a dislocated shoulder.

August 27, 1919 – Natal 3 NZ Army 17
Durban – Attendance 10,000

N – Try – Allan.

NZ – Tries – P W Storey 3, R Fogarty 2. Con – L B Stohr.

Natal included five players who toured New Zealand in 1921:

Walter Arthur Clarksen (three caps, 1921-24); L B Siedle (uncapped);

William Henry ('Taffy') Townsend (one cap, 1921); Alfred Percy Walker (six caps, 1921-24) and William C Zeller (two caps, 1921).

Townsend was a scrum half who had played in the King's Cup. He had been born in Newport (Wales) and was killed in action in Catania (Sicily) in WW2 at the age of 46 whilst serving as a private, then corporal, in the South African Infantry. He was a diamond digger.

September 3, 1919 – Western Province Universities 9 NZ Army 8
Newlands, Cape Town

WPU – J S de Kock, A J van Heerden, Roos.

NZ – Tries – R Fogarty, W A Ford. Con – L B Stohr.

Josias Servaas de Kock won two caps (1921-24) and toured New Zealand in 1921. Adrian Jacobus ('Attie') Van Heerden won two caps on the tour to New Zealand in 1921, then played rugby league for Wigan and Leigh. He took part in the 1920 and 1924 Olympic Games in the 440 yards hurdles.

For the tourists, McNaught retired with injury in the first half.

September 6, 1919 – Western Province 17 NZ Army 6
Cape Town

WP – Tries – Pienaar, A J van Heerden, H W Morkel. Cons – P G Morkel 2. DG – P G Morkel.

NZ – Try – W A Ford. Pen – E W Hasell.

Western Province v the 'All Blacks' Programme, Sept 6th 1919

The Morkels were full back Pieter Gerhard Morkel (eight caps, 1912-21) and the unrelated wing, Henry William Morkel (two caps, 1921). Both toured New Zealand in 1921 and 'PG' toured GB/France in 1912-13. De Kock and van Heerden had played in the previous game.

At this point, the tour became extended by extra games. The apparent explanation may lie in an interview given in 1965 by five-eighth G Jack McNaught. He recalled that there were record crowds at the matches, including one of 25,000. He declared the play was better than nowadays, with fewer line-outs, less kicking for touch and more open play. His side had lost the last game of the tour by 17-6 against Western Province, as they had become stale. Their departure was delayed, so they asked for a rematch and this game was one of the tour highlights. This time (see below) New Zealand won by as big a margin as they had lost previously.

September 12, 1919 – Western Province 3 NZ Army 20
Cape Town – Attendance 7,000

WP – Pen – P G Morkel.

NZ – Tries – **P W Storey 2, J A Bruce, R W Roberts. Cons – L B Stohr 4.

(** one try may have been scored by E L J Cockcroft).

'PG' Morkel again appeared against the tourists.

September 16, 1919 – Natal 4 NZ Army 11
Durban

N – DG – W H Townsend.

NZ – Tries – J A Bruce, E L J Cockcroft, unknown. Con – L B Stohr.

By contrast, this second clash with Natal ended with an almost identical result. 'Taffy' Townsend had also played for the hosts in the first meeting. The name of the player who scored by gathering a rebound off a home player was unknown.

No meeting took place with a full South African XV, and in fact the two countries did not meet at test level until 1921. However, it was this tour by the Services side that stirred South Africa and its rugby public to the enthusiasm for the game again and not only helped improve South African players, particularly in tackling and forward play, but gave the country a whole new impetus and desire to tour New Zealand as quickly as possible.

The 'Services All Blacks' finally reached New Zealand on the MS Ajana on October 16, 1919, but this was still not quite the end. They defeated Auckland by 19-6 before dispersing at last to their homes, but in May 1920 reassembled and, with 'Ranji' Wilson joining them, defeated Wellington by 23-8.

The Springboks went to New Zealand two years later for a drawn series which set up their long-lasting rivalry. Back to Mr Thomson's 'Words of

Passage': *'Percy Storey went on to play in the first two tests against the 1921 Boks, and in the first scored the final try to give the All Blacks a 13-5 victory. He played with an injured shoulder in the second test, won 9-5 by South Africa, and missed the scoreless mudbath of the third.*

In that game, Billy Fea played at first five-eighth inside the redoubtable former Rugby League exponent, Karl Ifwersen, and as well as Storey and Fea, the 1919 King's Cup winners were represented in the 1921 series by 'Moke' Belliss, J E Moffitt, R Fogarty and Alf West. Those four were all forwards in the toughest 2-3-2 formation of NZ tradition, and West toured Britain again in 1924-5.'

Sadly, it was not only the rivalry which was established. The Springboks were an all-white team due to South Africa's official policy of racial segregation, but the All Black team included several Maori players. During the tour the Springboks also played a game against an all-Maori 'Native' team, causing outrage in South Africa. It was the start of a 60-year battle between supporters and opponents of racial exclusion in rugby: and nearly 75 before Nelson Mandela's 'Rainbow Nation' lifted the real World Cup of Rugby.

Souvenir Programme, first SA tour of NZ, 1921

Meanwhile, the Australian Imperial Forces team had left England in May 1919 on RMS Orentes and arrived in Australia in July 1919. In South Africa on the way home the AIF defeated Natal 34-3 at Durban, but Beith, Carroll, Cody and Hickey were not with the team (see previous King's Cup biographies).

They returned to their homeland having established quite a global reputation: but with the NSWRU and their Queensland counterparts in disarray due to their decision to disband for the war, an East Coast exhibition tour was hastily organised for the first AIF. The internal tour ultimately saved the NSWRU from dissolving.

The AIF played eight more matches and won them all – New South Wales 42-14 (July 5); an Australian XV 28-18 at University Oval (July 12); Queensland 38-7 at Brisbane (July 19); an Australian XV 38-7; Queensland

AIF 30-3 at Brisbane (July 23); an Australian XV 27-18 (or 20-13) at Brisbane; North-West Union 56-3 (or 52-6!) at Inverek and an Australian XV 22-6 (August 2).

Some records suggested they played a further eight matches and won four, but though it cannot be fully verified it seems likely that it was the AIF second team, who lost to New South Wales 2nds 11-25 (July 5) and beat New England 35-11 at Adelaide (July 15).

However as most of the returning rugby stars were from NSW, the QRU didn't receive the same injection of players back into their ranks and they dissolved in 1920. They did not reform until 1928, explaining why it was the NSW Waratahs alone who returned to tour Britain in 1927.

Like the New Zealanders, they had their memories of the war and the peace, their scars from both rugby and battle field, their firm friendships and broadened horizons: but unlike their antipodean friend and rivals, they didn't have the King's Cup – the first World Cup? – in their locker.

The NZ press cutting from 1930 underlines, a decade on, the sense of importance and achievement attached to the winning of the trophy.

THE A.I.F. RUGBY UNION FOOTBALL TEAM OF 1919. THE ARROW SUPPLEMENT, 18/7/19.

Back Row: Corp. Stenning (N.S.W.), Sergt. G. Horsey (N.S.W.), Sergt. W. Bradley (N.S.W.), Corporal Dunn N.S.W.), Lieutenant W. O'Toole (N.S.W.), Lieutenant E. A. Cody (N.S.W.), and T. H. Bosward (the referee). Second Row: Gunner Rankin (Victoria), C.S.M. P. Buchanan (N.S.W.), Lieutenant W. T. Watson, M.C. and Bar and D.C.M. (N.S.W., capt.), Major W. F. Matthews (N.S.W., manager), Sergt. S. Egan (Queensland), Lance-Corporal J. Thompson (Q.), Gunner J. H. Bosward (N.S.W.). Front Row: Lieutenant Pountney (N.S.W.), Private J. Flanagan (Q.), Sergt. G. See (N.S.W.), Sergt. D. Suttor (N.S.W.), and Q.M.S. Bond (N.S.W.). The only team to defeat New Zealand, the winners of the Inter-Services Competition for the King's Cup

Australian Imperial Forces Rugby Team, July 1919

It remains to this day 'Down Under', belongs to the New Zealand Rugby Union, and fittingly, the Cup which George V presented for the Imperial Forces tournament continues to be used by the NZ Defence Force as the rugby trophy for their inter-services competition.

It took nearly 70 years before the opposition of many Unions was overcome and a first official World Cup was staged in 1987 – in New Zealand and Australia, and won by David Kirk's All Blacks. After several near misses they won it again at home in 2011, and sought to retain it in England in the autumn of 2015.

Typically. The All Blacks and their supporters were quick to nickname the RWC's William Webb Ellis Trophy 'Bill': it is not reported whether the King's Cup presented by the monarch in 1919 has ever been referred to as 'George'!

ARMY RUGBY TEAM
SUCCESSFUL REUNION
FUTURE OF THE KING'S CUP

Memories of the inter-Service Rugby football competition played in England in 1918 for the King's Cup were revived at a reunion last evening of the New Zealand Army Service team which won the coveted trophy. The reunion was the first since the team disbanded in 1919.

Mr. C. Brown (New Plymouth), who was captain of the team, presided, and other members of the team present were Messrs. A. F. Bellis, A. Bruce, M. Cain, W. R. Fea, W. Ford, A. Gilchrist, E. W. Hasell, W. L. Henry, J. Kissick, J. Moffitt, D. Sandman, S. J. Standen, and A. West. The gathering was a large one, and the proceedings were most cordial.

The following toasts were honoured: "The King," "Absent Members," "Army and Great War," "Army Team," and "The New Zealand and Wellington Rugby Unions."

The opinion was expressed that the King's Cup, which is now in Wellington, should be placed in the Memorial Hall to be erected on the Mount Cook site.

Several speakers stressed the desirability of members of the team keeping in touch with each other, and it was decided to hold similar gatherings on special occasions such as Rugby Test matches and other notable events.

A presentation was made to Mr. D. S. N. M'Cartney for his work in organising the function.

The Army team put up a great record in winning the King's Cup, and later, when it toured South Africa at the invitation of the authorities there, it did much to establish New Zealand's reputation for high-class Rugby.

Postscript - From the Trenches to the Playing Fields

'To show I could still do it'

As rugby at home looked to become fully restored at all levels, the memorials went up, the International Championship restarted in Britain in 1919-20 and continued until it was once again halted by conflict following the 1938-39 season.

While I cannot claim to have spoken to pre-WW1 players, my uncle, Wickham James Powell, did play four times for Wales in 1920 and I saw and met many who played in WW2. I can never forget speaking at his bedside on several occasions to Sid Hinam, the old Wales forward of 1925 and 1926.

He would have played with and against some of the King's Cup representatives, many of whom went on to win more – or like CSM Charles Jones and others, first – caps, in 1920 and after.

Sid had been in the Royal Artillery and the importance of rugby in his life showed when in our first meeting, with Sid bedbound and using an oxygen cylinder, he became excited as he relived his career. His wife said that I must go as he was gasping for breath. Sid reacted by taking the mask off and saying: *"If I die it must be talking rugby to Howard!"*

RFU Twickenham: War Memorial

27 fallen England Caps, 1914-1918

I also remember going to the house of Walter Vickery, the 1938 and 1939 Wales forward, whose father had been capped by England. I asked why, with dreadful hand and knee injuries before and during WW2, he had still skippered Aberavon in 1945-46 – ten years after he had last done so. Walter said: *"It was to show everyone I could still do it after the war years. But truly I couldn't, really, yet I soldiered on and then retired."*

It was that attitude that many had when returning from either war after huge gaps in their playing careers. They had lost five or six of the best years of their life and tried desperately to make up for them by playing again. Some players were relatively ageing when they finally went up to the

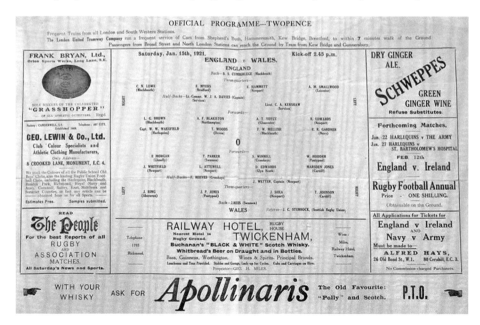

Some of the survivors play on: England v Wales 1921

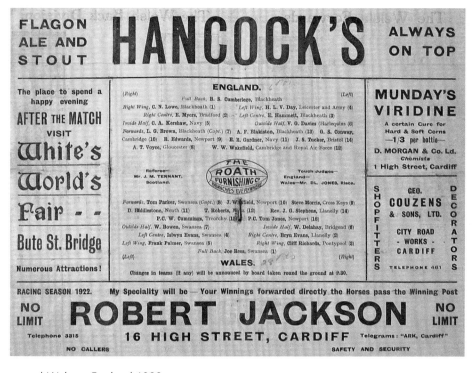

...and Wales v England 1922

universities they would have reached much earlier, had not their country called on them first.

Amongst the many reasons that hooked me on both rugby union and league was the thrill: of watching that mixture of old and new on the field; of marching out of grounds and down the roads with the supporters of both sides all together in one happy band; and of Walter Vickery's answer to my question: *"Was it all worth it if you had known of your injuries?"*

Walter put his hand inside his jacket and touched an old shirt, saying: *"To wear the red jersey was worth all that."* That was what made rugby union so special to me, especially in the late 1940s, after WW2.

So it must have been with many young men after 1918, with the crowds pouring in to see rugby in Britain, New Zealand and South Africa: though Australian union men were still battling against the very popular Aussie Rules football and rugby league in that country.

And so, the King's Cup had helped reinstate rugby union on these shores, although, as almost always, New Zealand were the best and fittest team with a winning habit, who had carried off this early – and only – attempt at a 'World Cup'.

Britain had to wait another five years to see the All Blacks here again, when Alf West alone returned as Cliff Porter's side enhanced the New Zealanders' mystique with the 'Invincible' tour of 1924-5.

South Africa's Springboks were not to return until 1931, and while both the Maoris and the NSW Waratahs sent good teams in the 1920s, those unfortunates, the Australian Wallabies chosen for their 1939-40 tour, arrived by sea on September 2, 1939, only to find war had been declared 24 hours later.

Ten days on, the Australian manager was telling a farewell lunch at Twickenham: *'We have one job in front of us now, to return and get into Australian uniforms without delay'*.

It was just 20 years since the King's Cup had supposedly helped mark the end of the 'war to end all wars'...

Appendix

Other Rugby Fixtures of Note: January to May 1919

January 13 – Leicester 0 New Zealand Services 19 (at Welford Road, Leicester).

Leicester – Frank Read; +Harold Day, C D Carter, Myley Abraham, *Percy Lawrie (capt); +Edward Myers, *Pedlar Wood; C D Ferris, Gordon Vears, *William Collopy, *Arthur Bull, Captain J Woolley, +F (Sos) Taylor, Jimmy Allen, *George Ward.

January 15 – Public Schools XV 0 New Zealand Trench XV 26 (at Old Deer Park, Richmond).

February 1 – Monmouthshire 3 New Zealand 'All Blacks' 22 (at Pandy Park, Cross Keys). The home side was made up mostly of Cross Keys players, including Ossie Male at full back and Stan Winmill in the forwards.

February 5 – Royal Naval Depot (Devonport) 3 Maoris 6 (at Devonport).

February 8 – Swansea 3 Maoris 10 (at St Helen's, Swansea). Swansea outside half Joe Fowler, who later turned to rugby league, kicked a goal from a mark. Maoris tries came from Sergeant (later Lieut) Walter Pukauae (Wattie) Barclay, MM and Lieutenant Gardener. Both were converted by Lieutenant Hohepa (Harry) Jacob, MM (All Black 1920).

February 8 – United Services 0 New Zealand 'All Blacks' 9 (at Torquay).

February 15 – Llanelli 6 Maoris 0 (at Stradey Park, Llanelli) (7,000). Llanelli – Try by wing Islwyn Evans (Wales, 4 caps 1922) and penalty by full back Hugh Jones. Swansea's Joe Fowler guested at outside half and the pack includesd Rev William Thomas Havard (Wales, 1 cap 1919) and Rev J C Thomas, as well as David Daniel (Dai) Hiddlestone (Wales, 5 caps 1922-24).

February 22 – Llanelli 9 New Zealand Machine Gun Corps 3 (at Stradey Park, Llanelli).

February 22 – Cardiff 0 New Zealand (Torquay-based) **XV 0** (at Arms Park, Cardiff).

February 22 – Coventry 0 New Zealand Reserves 13 (at Coventry).

March 15 – Cambridge Navy XV 16 Cambridge University 3. This was the first game at Cambridge since 1914. The Navy side were all naval officers in residence at the University.

March 19 – United Hospitals 0 Canadian Services 0 (at Honor Oak Park, home of Metropolitan Water Board).

March 19 – RAF 0 New Zealand Services 3 (at Richmond).

March 22 – RAF 13 United Hospitals 0 (at Richmond Athletic Ground).

March 22 – Gloucester 12 New Zealand Services 15 (at Kingsholm, Gloucester).

March 22 – Mother Country 28 Public Schools 0 (at Old Deer Park, Richmond).

March 29 – Cardiff 0 New Zealand Services 0 (at Arms Park, Cardiff) (10,000).

April 2 – Maesteg 3 New Zealand Services 8 (at Llynfi Road, Maesteg).

April 12 – Pill Harriers from Newport played their 27th successive unbeaten match with 26 wins and now a **0-0 draw** against a very strong **New Zealand Services 'B' XV** (10,000).

April 12 – Devon County 3 Australian Services 11 (at Exeter).

April 18-19 – These two days provided a good example of the overseas teams in action, as **Llanelli** beat **Canada 31-6** and scored seven tries, then defeated **United Services 20-3** the following day, while **Canada lost 6-19** at Kingsholm, **Gloucester**. **A New Zealand Egyptian Expeditionary Force XV won 21-3** at **Cardiff** Arms Park; **New Zealand Reserves won** at The Gnoll, **Neath 15-3**; **Australian Services beat** a combined **Exeter/Exmouth XV 9-3** (at Exmouth) and **a Wales XV drew 3-3** against the **38th Welsh Division** (at St Helen's, Swansea).

April 19 – Leicester 8 RAF 22 (at Welford Road, Leicester).

The **New Zealand Services** announced that after the King's Cup they would play five more games and their reserve team also would play five. Their reserves' record in Wales included victories over **Abertillery, 3-0 (April 5), Cross Keys, 6-0 (April 9)** and **Ogmore Vale, 12-7 (April 16).**

April 21 – The RAF began a short 'tour' of Wales, **defeating Neath 8-3** at The Gnoll (8,000).

April 21 – Pill Harriers 12 Australian Services 3 (at Newport).

April 21 – Bristol 6 A New Zealand XV (from Cosford) 10.

April 21 – Leicester 5 Mother Country 8 (at Welford Road, Leicester). Leicester – Try/Con – George Ward. Mother Country – Tries – R C W Pickles, W S Cullen. Con – B S Cumberlege.

April 22 – Llanelli 13 RAF 10 (at Stradey Park, Llanelli).

April 22 – Cross Keys 0 New Zealand Services 20 (at Bailey Park, Abergavenny).

The NZ Reserve XV at Abertillery, April 1919

April 23 – Abertillery 3 Australian Services 11 (at Abertillery Park).

April 23 – New Zealand Services fielded two sides, **defeating Ebbw Vale 28-0** (at Bridge End Park, Ebbw Vale) and **Coventry 47-0** (at Coventry).

April 26 – Llanelli 17 A New Zealand XV (from Larkhill) **9** (at Stradey Park, Llanelli).

April 26 – New Zealand Services fielded two sides **defeating Queen's University, Belfast 18-0** (at Belfast) and **United Services 20-7** (at Salisbury).

April 26 – Swansea 3 RAF 0 (at St Helen's, Swansea).

May 3 – Cornwall County 0 Australian Services 9 (at Camborne).

May 3 – Llanelli 17 Australian Services 3 (at Stradey Park, Llanelli).

May 3 – New Zealand Services fielded two sides **defeating Devon County 14-0** (at Torquay) and **drawing with Cardiff 3-3** (at Arms Park, Cardiff).

May 4 – France XV 10 New Zealand Expeditionary Forces 16 (at Stade Colombes, Paris).

May 5 – Monmouthshire 4 New Zealand Services 3 (at the Bridge End Field, Ebbw Vale). Wales cap Jerry Shea (Pill Harriers) dropped a goal to win it after forward Eric J Naylor had scored the New Zealand try.

May 8 – Selection Francaise 6 New Zealand Expeditionary Forces 16 (at Toulouse).

May 10 – Northern Command 0 New Zealand Services 33 (at Headingley) in aid of St Dunstan's Hostel for Blinded Soldiers and Sailors.

Overall in the calendar year **1919** the **New Zealand Services** were credited with **33 wins**, **two losses** (**Australia** in the King's Cup and **Monmouthshire**) and three draws (**Cardiff, Pill Harriers** and the **Royal Navy Division**), all ending **0-0**.

Other wins by the **New Zealand Service** teams included a **GB XV, 11-3 (at Welford Road, Leicester)** and **Tredegar, 8-0.**

Meanwhile, legendary rugby league centre **Harold Wagstaffe** played for the RASC and 2nd Lt. **Tommy Voyce** of the Royal West Kent Regiment appeared for a Home Army XV. He went on to win 27 England caps (1920-26), despite being wounded in one eye while serving in the Gloucestershire Regiment in WW1. In WW2 he was a major in the RASC.

A tournament was played at **Aldershot** in **April 1919** between three teams, the **BEF** (the British Expeditionary Forces in France) winning over Egypt (**the New Zealanders from Egypt**) and the **Home Forces**. It was dubbed the 'Theatre of War Championship'.

April 23 – Egypt 6 Home Forces 0. Lieutenant Scott of the Wellington Mounted Rifles scored a try and a penalty.

April 26 – BEF 6 Home Forces 3. Tries by Captain Ferguson of the London Regiment and Major Harrison of the Royal Garrison Artillery against a try by Lieutenant Willerson of the Machine Gun Corps.

April 28 – BEF 5 Egypt 3. Major Harrison scored a try converted by Alexander William Angus, DSO (Scotland, 18 caps, 1909-20) against a try by McNeill.

As well as playing in the King's Cup and the matches previously detailed, the **Australian Imperial Forces** also defeated the **South African Forces, 9-8** (at Queen's Club, West Kensington); **Royal Navy Devonport, 14-10** and **Maesteg 18-3,** but lost to **Ogmore Vale 3-6.**

The **Australian Trench team** won five games and lost four, including wins by **17-0** against **Llanelli** at Stradey Park **(March 15)** and **27-11** against **East Midlands** at Northampton **(March 29).**

Select Bibliography

Phil Atkinson: *100 Years of Rhymney Rugby* (1982)
John Billot: *All Blacks in Wales* (1972), *Springboks in Wales* (1974)
Rod Chester & Nev McMillan: *Encyclopedia of New Zealand Rugby* (1981)
Tony Collins: *Rugby Union & the First World War, Historical Journal* (Dec. 2002)
Stephen Cooper: *The Final Whistle* (2012)
Stephen Cooper: *After the Final Whistle* (2015)
Danny Davies: *Cardiff RFC History & Statistics* (1976)
W J A Davies: *Rugby Football* (1923)
Stuart Farmer & David Hands: *Tigers -The Official History of Leicester Football Club* (1993 & 2014)
John M. Jenkins, Duncan Pierce & Tim Auty: *Who's Who of Welsh International Rugby Players* (1991)
Ira Jones: *An Air Fighter's Scrapbook* (1938)
Peter Lawless: *Rugger's An Attacking Game* (1946)
Steve Lewis: *Newport Rugby Football Club 1874-1950* (1999)
John Mace: *The History of the Royal Air Force Rugby 1919-1999* (2000)
Winston McCarthy: *Broadcasting with the Kiwis* (1947)
Jack Pollard: *Australian Rugby Players* (1994)
Gwyn Prescott: *'this rugby spellbound people'* (2011 & 2015), *'Call Them to Remembrance'* (2014)
Mike Price: *Neath RFC 1871 - 1945* (2002)
Huw Richards: *A Game for Hooligans* (2006)
Peter Sharpham: *The First Wallabies* (2000)
Dai Smith & Gareth Williams: *Fields of Praise* (1980)
Doug Sturrock: *Files courtesy of the Honorary Historian of BC Rugby*
John Bell Thomson: *Words of Passage: The Original* (2012)
A M C Thorburn: *Official History of the SRU* (1985)
W W Wakefield: *Rugger* (1927)

Newspapers
The Times: Issues between 1915 and 1919

Websites
Tony Collins: *Rugby Reloaded* (Internet Blog 2014-15)
Wikipedia: *Britain in 1919*

ST DAVID'S PRESS

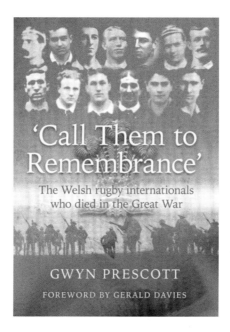

'These pages contain an unexplored and untold tale which, from the deepest anguish of the suffering born of their unquestioning bravery, pierces the heart...This book is [an] acknowledgment of the sacrifice made by 13 Welshmen....Theirs was a sacrifice which needs to be told....Gwyn Prescott, with meticulous and sympathetic attention to detail, tells the story. This narrative is an essential record'.
Gerald Davies, from the Foreword

'From the boisterous singing and exhilarating cheers of Cardiff Arms Park to the deafening roar of artillery shells and gunfire, these humbling stories describe thirteen individual journeys which began on muddy yet familiar Welsh playing fields but ended in the unimaginable brutality of the battles of the First World War.'
Dan Allsobrook, www.gwladrugby.com

'This is a book which moves as well as informs.'
Huw Richards, Associate Lecturer in Sports History, London College of Communication

978 1 902719 375 - £14.99 - 175pp - 120 illustrations/photographs

ST DAVID'S PRESS

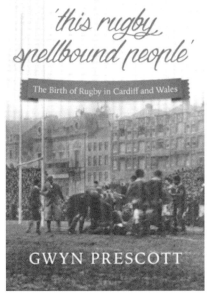

this rugby spellbound people

The Birth of Rugby in Cardiff and Wales

GWYN PRESCOTT

"...*scrupulously researched [and] well written ...Gwyn Prescott has given [rugby in Wales] a history to be proud of.*
"**Huw Richards,** *scrum.com*

"*Gwyn Prescott paints a meticulous picture of Welsh rugby's growth in Victorian Britain.*
"**Rugby World**

"*It's a fascinating piece of research and a major contribution to the history of rugby, not just in Wales but generally.*
"**Tony Collins, author of** *A Social History of English Rugby Union*

"*If rugby is your thing...then get yourself a copy of Gwyn Prescott's account of the social, cultural and economical impact of rugby football on the people of South Wales...a detailed and fascinating study of the way in which rugby embedded itself in the fabric of Cardiff society and the villages and towns of South Wales, transforming itself from a fringe activity confined to the middle classes, to the mass-participation sport it became in the twentieth-century.*
"**Gwladrugby.com**

"*the most assiduous archival research and rigorous command of the skills of the social historian...a book that also has significant implications for the historiography of rugby...*
"**Sport in History**

"*I knew immediately that I would enjoy Gwyn Prescott's account of how the game of rugby not only came to Cardiff but conquered it...The details are richly satisfying...The story is engrossing... If you have any nostalgia for those days when one eagerly crossed Westgate Street to get to a game this is the book for you.*
"**Peter Stead**

978 1 902719 436 - £14.99 - 304pp - 142 illustrations/photographs

St David's Press

SPIKEY
2
HARD TO HANDLE
The Autobiography of Mike 'Spikey' Watkins
with Anthony Bunko

one of the most inspirational leaders that Welsh rugby has ever produced'
Mike Ruddock

' ...a great friend...also a great inspiration...he led from the front and his team mates could always rely on him when things got a bit rough....even though he'd probably started it!!'
Paul Turner, from the Foreword

'No one trained harder, no one played harder...heart of a lion, small in stature with a giant's presence'
Terry Holmes

'Spikey Watkins is the most 'Rock 'n' Roll' Welsh Sportsman ever. The establishment hated him but the people loved him. This is the best sports autobiography I've ever read. Buy or steal a copy now'
Jonathan Owen

One of the most colourful and controversial characters in Welsh rugby history, Mike 'Spikey' Watkins remains the only player since 1882 to captain Wales on his debut, and win.

Discarded by Cardiff RFC and banned by the WRU after the infamous 'Hookers Night Out' incident in November 1978, Spikey, who had regularly played for the Wales B team and was understudy to Bobby Windsor in the great Welsh team of the 1970s, thought his chance of a prized Welsh cap has disappeared.

In this brutally frank and hard-hitting autobiography, 'Spikey' Watkins, the loveable rogue of Welsh rugby, lifts the lid on his roller-coaster playing career and explains how he fought back against the 'blazer-brigade' he despised, returned to captain a hugely successful Newport team and finally got the call from the WRU, due to public pressure from the supporters who adored him, to captain his country to victory against Ireland in 1984.

978 1 902719 405 - £18.99 - 224pp - 24pp illustrations/photographs